Invisible Rendezvous

Invisible Rendezvous: Connection and Collaboration in the New Landscape of Electronic Writing

Rob Wittig for IN.S.OMNIA

Wesleyan University Press
Published by University Press of New England
Hanover and London

Wesleyan University Press

Published by University Press of New England, Hanover, NH 03755

© 1994 by Rob Wittig

All rights reserved

Printed in the United States of America 5 4 3 2 1

CIP data appear at the end of the book

IN.S.OMNIA wishes to thank the Fulbright Collaborative Research Program and our Fulbright sponsors, Jacques Derrida, Jean-François Lyotard, and Marc Girard of the Centre Georges Pompidou, for their kind assistance in the development of this book.

Contents

Foreword by Philip Wohlstetter ix

exempli gratia i 1

Chapter 1 If a New World Were Discovered 2

exempli gratia ii 10

Chapter 2 Restless Nights in the Electronic City: What is IN.S.OMNIA? 16

exempli gratia iii 29

Chapter 3 This Region We Invent and Defend: Mapping the Invisible 42

exempli gratia iv 49

Chapter 4 Learning to Write Algorithmically: The Novel Project 64

exempli gratia v 78

Chapter 5 Sampling and Linking: IN.S.OMNIA and the Habits of Hypertext 86

exempli gratia vi 96

Chapter 6 From Messages to Projects: New Genres for a New Geography 106

exempli gratia vii 120

Chapter 7 Anyone Can Play, Pro or Am: Tapping Everyday Creativity 126

Exempli gratia viii 133

Chapter 8 Acknowledging Collaboration: New Roles for Writers 136

exempli gratia ix 146

Chapter 9 Doing Voices: Since Each of Us Was Several 150

exempli gratia x 158

Chapter 10 Astonish Us! 168

References 173

Credits 178

Index 183

Foreword

Homer, you say, is the first Great Author? The man whose mastery of the new technology of writing allowed him to re-read, to revise, to impose an artistic unity on a thousand years of anonymous oral tradition?

By all means let us try and imagine this process.

We are in eighth century Ionia. Writing in this time and place employs a wooden tablet with a waxed surface (the support) and a sharp wooden stick (the inscribing tool). "Homer" begins to write—but what? A transcription of his last performance? How can he remember it exactly since it varies each time? Let's say he starts to perform and writes as he goes "Menin aeide, thea . . ." (Pauses to write.) Μῆνιν 'άειδε, θεά. Course if he keeps pausing to write it down, he's not going to improvise much of a performance.

Okay, he hires a scribe with very, very, very quick hands. Fair enough. They cancel all their appointments for two weeks and produce a transcription. A first draft. Not on typewriter paper, remember, but on (conservatively) seven or eight hundred wooden tablets that are, let's say, piled up in a large wooden box. Time to revise now. No page numbers, folks, but Homer (being a Genius) has devised an ingenious filing system that allows (after a bit of shuffling) access to any part of the poem he wants to work on. But wait a minute, he's blind! Okay, okay, okay, so he does the tablets in Braille . . .

Not too long ago, we invented a city. We set out out in search of it and (happy accident) we landed somewhere else. The city was called Invisible Seattle. The city of Seattle—the visible city—was merely a subset of this wider realm, which included recognizable fragments of Paris, Ionia, and Tlon in accordance with our slogan "Every time you read a book, you enter Invisible Seattle." We—the individuals involved in this surprisingly addictive enterprise—made every effort to impose our collective dream on the civic unconscious through a series of dada-inspired performance pieces: Trials of the Enemies of Civic Life, for example, or ceremonial renamings of city streets. "The city and all of its structures are 'found objects,' " we wrote in one of our manifestoes, "not created by you or me, but capable of being re-created . . . If the slogan of the modern movement is 'Form Follows Function,' Invisible Seattle's is 'Function Follows Fiction.' "

One summer, dressed as "Literary Workers" in hard hats and white overalls, we roamed the streets gathering words and texts from passersby. These texts (a kind of modern, freeze-dried version of Homeric oral tradition) were compiled into a novel on a gigantic literary computer called Scheherezade II. The project was entitled "The Novel of Seattle by Seattle." Out of it arose an electronic bulletin board accessible by phone line to any writer with a computer and a modem.

Thus almost by accident was IN.S.OMNIA born—the "Invisible Rendezvous" that all the time lay in wait for us (for you, Dear Reader and Writer). It is this space which Literary Worker Rob Wittig and the "invisibles" explore, catalog, and speculate about in the chapters and "examples" of this marvelous book. But the book concerns itself less with the technology per se than with finding ways to conceptualize this new site of writing.

At the very least, it is another mode of publishing. An ideal writing laboratory. Site for Oulipean games, collaborative ventures within agreed-upon formal structures, warming-up exercises before the return to the more traditionally-conceived, solitary literary pursuit, which continues to exist side by side, though mysteriously altered.

In its most visionary incarnation, it is an electronic town square. A true Republic of Letters. Literature without Names.

At its most insistent, it is an invitation to rethink everything we seem to know about the Book and Writing and Literature and how these all fit together.

It is easy to keep telling ourselves the same old lies. That all Great Books are written by God (generally appearing in the guise of Genius or Inspiration to his deputy on earth, the Great Author). Don't ask how. Just believe that they are created in one seamless spiritual instant. That there is nothing accidental in them. That every word, every comma mirrors the perfection of the Divine Order. Etcetera.

But how much more interesting to root ourselves in the primal stuff, the dense matter of writing.

The alphabet of the stars, says Mallarmé, is written luminously on a dark field, but man must write in black on white pages. Not any more. Now we write and read luminous text on a dark screen. "Ecriture" from the Black Lagoon.

We as writers can still ask ourselves familiar questions. Is this idea a short story or a novel? Do I write it in the first, second, or third person? But we can no longer avoid asking others. What site does my writing seek? What technology of inscription should I employ? What support? Paper? The ephemeral cathode ray tube? The semi-eternality of stone?

If we can barely imagine how the first work of our literature was put together, let us, at least, reserve our judgment as to where and by what process the next one might emerge.

Welcome to the world of connection, collaboration, craft, contingency, and glorious confusion.

New pleasures and new vices await you.

Philip Wohlstetter

----

exempli gratia i

. . . if a new world were discovered today, would we be able to *see* it? Would we be able to clear from our minds the images we habitually associate with our expectations of a different world (those of science fiction, for example) to grasp the real difference that lay before our eyes? (Calvino 1984, 15)

chapter 1

If a New World Were Discovered

I85jan18 from Grothus
The invention of the fishhook was preceded by the invention of the letter "J."
And the fishnet was invented by a fisherman who was reading the fisherman's
bible and noticed that all the words he'd been reading were like little fishes,
caught in the reticulation of spaces between them.I

I85jan19 from Bill Williams
The "empty book" was written by a man who had read a lot of full books and
noticed that in many of them the spaces were caught by the little nets made by
the words. (IN.S.OMNIA)I

This exchange took place no place. That is to say, it took place in multiple places. It took place on the bright screens of spanking new personal computers, on the dim screens of junky dumb terminals with second-hand modems. Cats rubbed against this exchange as they investigated the human's new toy plunked on the kitchen table. It flowed through phone lines and satellite links, it was printed out on paper in various locations at various times. At the center of all this activity was a machine called IN.S.OMNIA, an electronic town square, sitting up all night, recording and recalling texts from its digital memory.

The IN.S.OMNIA electronic bulletin board, founded in 1983, is a venue for the exchange of alphanumeric characters. Users have described it as a digital coffeehouse, a place of refuge where they can be their various selves, a non-place on which to stand and survey the other zones—books, billboards, brochures—where texts operate.

What is interesting about IN.S.OMNIA is not that it is unique but that it is typical. IN.S.OMNIA is not avant-garde in the old-fashioned sense. It is a representative hunk of end-of-the-century culture—representative in its informal form, its clashing content, and its collaborations. Regular callers to IN.S.OMNIA (we call ourselves in.s.omniacs) find the displaced experience of posting pseudonymous texts on the system to be eerily normal, even familiar. In.s.omniacs have come to understand that their electronic experiences are indicative of a world of unrecognized esthetic practices.

In.s.omniacs themselves are typical examples of the large, unseen world of "cultural activists" spread across the continent. Without pausing to obtain the authorization of the mainstream, these activists simply spend what money and free time they have on the impassioned production of objects, events, and publications.

These independents share a transdisciplinary diversity of education and work experience, being "culture vultures" of one stripe or another, but rarely are they the products of formal writing or fine arts programs. Staying true to a kind of cultural common sense, they engage in activities that seem interesting and funny and right, even though these activities evolve away from rewarded definitions of "serious art."

Like in.s.omniacs, most of these generous squanderers of talent and energy have a proclivity for working in groups. Their attitude finds no useful distinction between "high" and "low" art and no opposition between nature and artifice. These postindustrialists accept the fact that their surroundings "naturally" contain commercials and celebrities alongside trees and streams. For them, an image is no less real than its model, only different. The image is a real image, and its practical effect on the world must be understood and taken seriously. New technologies inspire neither reflexive fear nor automatic enthusiasm but are evaluated on the basis of what they can do for the project at hand.

Viewed by the mainstream as primal, expressive, and unselfconscious, these activists are, in fact, tireless historians and scholars. Aware of their connections to alternative traditions, they construct careful counterhistories and refusenik halls of fame. Those from theater backgrounds might point to Jarry, Artaud, Andy Kauffman, musicians to Gesualdo, Satie, Zappa. But whatever their education, the activists feel they have left the old disciplines behind. "I used to be a [insert writer, artist, dancer, etc.]," goes the familiar conversation. "I don't know what you'd call what I'm doing these days." The in.s.omniacs' background—our habitual blindness, our prison—is literary, a thread of modernism obsessed with the apocalyptic production of "the last book."

Underlying this activism is a basic cultural rationale. It is understood that there is an interplay between the structures of culture and the structures of life. It is possible for a form of culture—say, literature—to become out of sync with life and prepare people to recognize configurations of experience that are no longer relevant. Mainstream art no longer helps us navigate the world; we must find something better.

How does the universe of cultural activism manifest itself? A constant in the homes of all these creators (including in.s.omniacs) is a modern version of a *wunderkammer*, the medieval "room of marvels" in which was kept the jewelry, the piece of Chinese silk, the oil painting, the odd book, the toe of the saint. Today's *wunderkammer* take the form of shelves, drawers, or stacks full of photocopied pamphlets, raw flyers, postcards, fanzines, and paperbacks. From the self-published paper and acetate *Lines on Lines* by Kay Rosen (1982) to the program of the 1989 *Festival of Plagiarism* (Perkins), from the photographs of *Carkeek's Pocket Guide to Plywood Veneer Grades* published by New York's Feature Gallery (1990) to Marc Saporta's loose-leaf novel *Composition No. 1* (1962), from the dot matrix printout of *Between C and D* (1990) to a review of an installation called *The Legible City* (Spence 1993) in which readers sit on a bicycle interface watching a giant screen and touring typographic streets, from the laser printed cover of a home-compiled music cassette called *Phonic* (undated) to a photocopied nuptial announcement booklet entitled *Couple Weds in Bizarre Ceremony* (Wendy and Tom 1987), from a publicity packet for the film *Anne of the Thousand Days* (Universal Pictures 1970) to Nick Bantock's *Sabine's Notebook* (1992), from a suspiciously incompetent 1853 Philadelphia edition of Addison's *Spectator* to the transcript of a philosophical electronic bulletin board established for the exposition *Les Immatériaux* (CCI 1985), from the *National Lampoon's Sunday Newspaper Parody* (O'Rourke 1978) to the Church of the Subgenius's brochure that begins "Repent!! Quit your job! SLACK OFF!" (Subgenius Foundation 1981), such collections are treasured clues to a new kind of cultural production. To those who hoard them, these novelties—and the shape of the collections they create—correspond to the world more accurately than the 6x9" books in neat rows in the bookstore.

As the 1980s progressed, this sea of publications found its own bibliographers. Mike Gunderloy and Cari Goldberg's dense and encyclopedic *Factsheet Five* (1991) "the 'zine of crosscurrents and cross-pollination" contained page after page of reviews of other tiny 'zines, all with mailing addresses and subscription rates. Sections were devoted to music 'zines, cartoons, "one-shots" (nonserial publications) t-shirt reviews, artifact reviews (buttons, stickers, armbands, etc.), and even a "Hall of Shame" to rebuke recalcitrant micropublishers.

The Church of the Subgenius's own *High Weirdness by Mail: A Directory of the Fringe: Mad Prophets, Crackpots, Kooks & True Visionaries* is a monument to this kind of universal curiosity. Its spirit is summed up in a line the Subgenius's Rev. Ivan Stang A.Ø. shouted lustily at one of the church's "devivals," castigating the narrow-minded and the prudish (September 1992): "When a Subgenius sees something that offends and annoys and disturbs him he says to himself, 'Damn, that offends and annoys and disturbs me. I MUST FIND OUT MORE ABOUT IT!' "

What is this frenzy of publishing, collecting, cataloging? What are these labors of love—whose primary techniques are collage, travesty, and pastiche—but ways of coping with the tsunami of communication flooding us in the so-called "information age"?

⌐93jun24 from Thrilling Voice
We were trained for a future that never arrived.⌐

⌐93jun25 from Person
We were all packed up to transport our old habits to a new world. Instead, the new world quietly infiltrated the old one and now the two coexist. This renders our old, single-world habits useless.⌐

⌐93jun27 from "Big Phone" Bill
That's it. What characterizes this age is that we are done with simple revolutions where one world replaces another. New worlds arrive but none of the old ones leave. Our everyday lives are crowded with ghosts.⌐

⌐93jun27 from Person
We are beyond travelling. Archiving plus telecommunications means that we are routinely in several places at once. Existing in more than one world at once is now the central phenomenon of our time. In fact we revel in the cheerful and impossible co-existence of mutually exclusive worlds.⌐

⌐93jun28 from Carpet Sample
Who's complaining? Minimum: two worlds at once. Anything less would be too fucking boring. (IN.S.OMNIA)⌐

Umberto Eco's *Foucault's Pendulum* (1989) is a meditation on the dilemma of what constitutes a "serious" text as opposed to a "marginal" or "crank" text. The Church of the Subgenius, a group that compiles every conspiracy theory it finds into one massive delirium, a group that operates only pseudonymously and never "breaks character" as it brags that it is "an inherently bogus religion that will tell you that you are better than everyone else," is *playing* in the same border zone Eco contemplates.

Gone are the days when the required books of a basic education could be counted in the hundreds and read in an adolescence. Millions of texts clamor for our attention. To make sense of them requires cunning, speed, and multileveled thinking. Sophisticated techniques of irony, punning, and collage are used for their efficiency. Quick acts of selection and linkage are the name of the game.

Some cultural activists use computer technology to practice these techniques, others don't. The distinction is unimportant. What is at stake here is not new technologies in themselves but new habits of mind. New technologies are a dime a dozen, ideas are always in short supply.

All the gregarious efforts of "cross-pollination" point out that the information age is at the same time a new dark age. Cultural activists usually feel isolated and seek out similar projects, like nuns and monks roaming from abbey to abbey in search of manuscripts. To publish small pieces in such a period is to call in the darkness for new companions, new collaborators.

Our unique issue of a bright orange magazine bearing the title *Invisible Seattle's Omnia* was such a call. In 1985 it found its way into a small number of *wunderkammer*. "This is not IN.S.OMNIA" its back cover proclaimed. "The document you hold is a bundle of paper inscribed with ink, a representation of the writing that appears on IN.S.OMNIA. IN.S.OMNIA exists on discs in a computer . . . IN.S.OMNIA is a forum for interactive literature, a mode of self-publishing that eliminates printing presses, paper, and publishers. Call, read, write . . . every reader is a writer, and new forms appear, a new writing that is at once literature, graffiti, conversation, and word games."

IN.S.OMNIA was at its origin *Invisible Seattle's Omnia*, a project of a group called Invisible Seattle. Founded by a collusion of writers, actors, and visual artists, the Invisible Seattle of the early '80s operated under the analogy of an alternate city government. In events that would have been described as "performance art," the group aired proclamations, conducted trials of "the enemies of civic life," and held Invisible Seattle city council meetings. Reminiscent of the readings and gatherings of the San Francisco Poetry Renaissance of the '50s, the "invisibles" held public meetings at a downtown coffeehouse and weekly salons in a Capitol Hill apartment.

> **In 1983, the Novel of Seattle project attempted to construct a city of words—or, rather, a city out of words—out of the words of its inhabitants, out of their narratives, memories, images—hoping that this "city of words" would eventually transform the visible city (as similar fictions have transformed other cities where people proudly point out that they live on the same block as Raskolnikov or Sherlock Holmes).**
>
> **For a month, "Literary Workers" wearing hard hats and white overalls prowled the streets reading the prologue and gathering texts from passersby . . . and these texts, a million utterances searching for their authentic environment, were compiled into a novel on a gigantic literary computer called Scheherezade II. (*Invisible Seattle's Omnia* 1985, 87)**

Soon after the Novel Project, in the studio of Scheherezade II's sculptor, a heap of junked computer equipment sprang into action as an electronic bulletin board. He offered the use of the system during the late night hours to the invisibles. IN.S.OMNIA was born.

The IN.S.OMNIA electronic bulletin board became the focus of the group's activities, and in the following years, as the participants dispersed around the country, it was the site of a series of textual investigations. By the end of the decade, no more events were being conducted under the name Invisible Seattle, but the on-again off-again work on IN.S.OMNIA was a hotbed for a handful of callers from all walks of life. Invisible Seattle's search for an alternate geography had produced the perfect non-place.

In 1987 two in.s.omniacs were dispatched to Paris on a mission to develop a plan for an extravagant, international project that combined the human geography of the early projects with the discoveries of the bulletin board. The result was *The Plan for Invisible America: More Than a Game—More Than a Novel, a Stupendous, Computer-Based, Bilingual, Transatlantic, Collaborative, History-Making Project* (*IN.S.OMNIA Print Outs* 1, 1987). The report spawned ideas from which have come a series of "IN.S.OMNIA Print Outs."

This decade of texts and events—culminating in the weather system of form and content that is IN.S.OMNIA—is the subject of this book.

The experience of writing on IN.S.OMNIA haunts its users. They have seen the inexorable sweep of incoming messages across their home screens. They have responded immediately in any of a number of pseudonymous voices, working in collaboration with unseen others on strange projects in as-yet-unnamed genres.

In.s.omniacs have other names, other lives in the "face world" beyond the bulletin board. IN.S.OMNIA is a mask anyone can don at will, a set of altered egos in which to re-experience the world. For most, IN.S.OMNIA remains a hidden vice, a literary sin, a perplexing fact of life that can't be pigeonholed.

IN.S.OMNIA is not literature as most of us learned it. It is too raw, too rambling, too dependent on timing and context. Its projects are too often planned but not executed, or commenced with enthusiasm only to languish when participants are drawn into their "face world" commitments. It is formally complex, making it difficult to discern beginnings and endings. Its projects frequently leave the electronic system altogether to migrate into other forms.

But IN.S.OMNIA is hard to forget. It persists, it insists. IN.S.OMNIA keeps coming up in our conversations as the best analogy for certain changes in the world. For pure joy we hunt down stellar passages in stacks of old IN.S.OMNIA printouts and read them aloud. IN.S.OMNIA wantonly violates the norms of proper literary behavior but has given us some of the best literary experiences of our lives. IN.S.OMNIA is important, and understanding it is important.

The society is programmed to look for the "next big thing" in literature. What if this time the next big thing is not a "hot young novelist" or even a mass migration from the technology of the printed book to the technology of screens and wires? What if the next big thing already surrounds us, embedded in small gestures we perform every day? What if the next big thing is the realization that we have changed the way we *use* culture—remapping, rewiring, renetworking the same old pool of elements in new ways, adding to them with furtive scribbles, seeking pleasures without naming them? What if that new way of using culture remains invisible because we have been taught to look for the wrong things—for authors, works, and readers? Meeting and working at the invisible rendezvous of IN.S.OMNIA has allowed us to glimpse these pleasures.

This book wonders aloud if these marginal, re-creational behaviors aren't poised to become the predominant cultural forms of the future.

It is not surprising that this is a book and not a computer program. Many of the people for whom this account is intended—cultural activists like us who play with the pieces of an unglued culture—can't afford computers. The distribution machine of trucks and bookstores is extensive and reliable. Reality is characterized by such anachronisms. Computer instructions come in books; the fax machine has revived handwriting; we stick Post-Its™ on our screens.

More important, what you hold in your hands is much more than a book. All books are. This is only the tip of a larger project consisting of years of phone calls, letters, meetings, electronic exchanges, and sumptuous dinners.

So, dear in.s.omniacs, we meet again behind the mask! This time a single mask, a single discursive voice, a single book we have jammed into like a phone booth with the goal of analyzing more than a decade of passionate wrangling. Dear Reader, pay no attention to the man behind the curtain; the voice you hear is not to be identified with the literary contractor who drew the short straw and whose name appears on the byline.

Our object here is more to ask than to tell. If readers like the notions they find here, we hope they will "Take our ideas. Please!" But our most fervent hope is that this smoke signal will allow us to meet the better bulletin boards, the more grandiose projects, the smarter groups that are surely out there gathering at their own invisible rendezvous.

exempli gratia ii

▌85mar09 from "Big Phone" Bill
Let's assume, for the sake of art, that the Barthes of "The Death of the Author" and the Derrida of "The End of the Book and the Beginning of Writing" are correct. NOW WHAT HAPPENS? That's what we're here to find out. (IN.S.OMNIA)▌

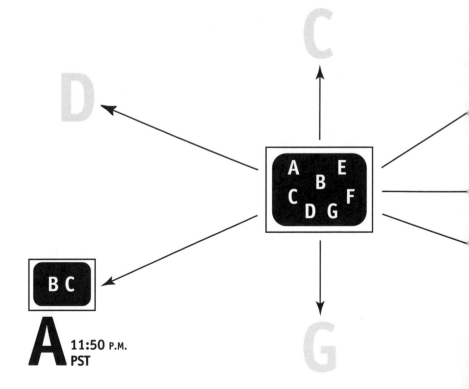

90july18 from our correspondent
Dateline Rural Virginia. The American countryside is no longer the fastness of On the Road or the gothic of Tennessee Ernie Williams. You walk into the office of Mockingbird Motel expecting the familiar aroma of mildew and Floral Bouquet soap. Instead you smell curry. The trilingual guy (how must HE view this little burg?) behind the counter pulls your receipt off the dot matrix printer. Every motel has cable. Which I don't even have at home in the Big City. I'm more in touch on the road than at home. News on tap, 24 hours a day. And The Weather Channel!

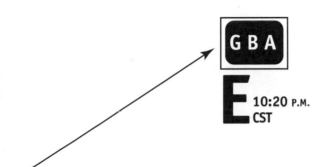

Where is IN.S.OMNIA? Users A, B, and E call the electronic bulletin board system one evening from their homes. IN.S.OMNIA "comes to" A, B, and E (bringing past users C, D, F, and G) just as the users "travel to" IN.S.OMNIA. They have met at a distant rendezvous without leaving the room. Users report feeling that they are "in" both places and neither.

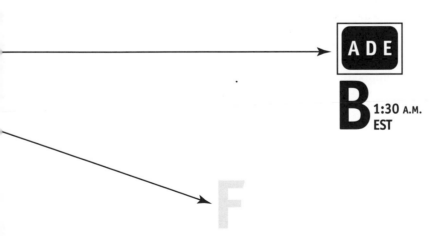

Every morning you see a live satellite picture, figure out where you are, watch the fronts bearing down—you don't even need a weatherperson to interpret. The Weather Channel is the most important thing on TV; as it is now, so shall all broadcasting someday be. You walk the Appalachian trail and hear a startlingly familiar call echoing in the woods. Some prodigious mockingbird. You come around a corner and there's an Indonesian visitor with his American host huddled around a dark object. A cellular phone. The sound was digital dialing. "Honey. Sorry to wake you up, but I'm on this incredible mountain, it's beautiful!" (IN.S.OMNIA)▌

▌9 2 j u n 1 1   f r o m   B e L o n g

Southwestern red light: Motel Desert Varnish, room unaccountably pie-wedge shaped, pink stucco walls with jade or likelier turquoise wainscotting; from the ceiling dangling . . . a mobile of glazed clay pigeons turning, dipping, cooing amorously in the air-conditioned updrafts, other more native and geometric arts & crafts motionless and receding to the artificial vanishing point, the distant fuzzy apex of the pigeon-pie gallery. I a lump of sex in bed, calling the purl of her name over and over through the dander of the thundershower she takes with her, along with her lost ceramic skills. The last recorded footstep on a terra-cotta moon clangs like a windchime, two porcelain birds colliding in a vacuum. (IN.S.OMNIA)▌

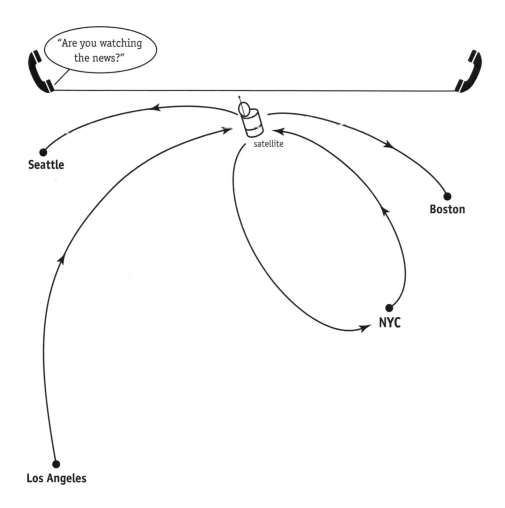

A typical telecommunications moment. A person in Seattle is talking with a retailer in Boston while watching a muted television displaying a live report of an emergency in Los Angeles. The Seattle caller hears a voice in the background of the Boston store that matches the announcer's lips moving on the Seattle screen. "Are you watching the news?" Both are tuned to the same broadcast (which is being coordinated in New York). The Boston and Seattle callers discuss and "attend" the Los Angeles event "together."

What the foreign community of Zyzzyzywa considers romantic, exotic adventure, the locals consider tedium. My only sport, my sole remaining vehicle for excitement, is to drive the Mercedes into Old Zyzzyzywa to scare the foreign community, who now are practically the old city's only inhabitants. Even the living quarters in the brothels have been "restored" into offices where the international press agencies and intelligence agencies (who claim they can tell each other apart some- how) have installed their microwave dishes and telex terminals to keep track of one another's activities. The working girls, just like the veg- etable merchants and the underpaid security staff such as myself, must commute at the end of the working day or night back to New Zyzzyzywa. The already deteriorating concrete-block apartment cubicle provided to me by the authorities was originally built to house the press and international business travelers in an attempt to prove that our embattled land was making that giant stride into the 20th century . . . when the then-new government began to receive complaints about New Zyzzyzywa from people wanting to stay in Old Zyzzyzywa to haggle with merchants, engage with aging transvestites, and listen to tradi- tional music. As all of the light entertainment programming on Radio Zyzzyzywa consisted then of local impersonations of French and Austrian band singers, a Ministry of Traditional Culture was formed to devise an instant cultural heritage in folk dance, literature, and music and to invent the instruments, printing techniques, and costumes to bring them to life. The ministry is housed in what was to have been the communications center in New Zyzzyzywa. All of the lower level domes- tic affairs departments are housed in New Zyzzyzywa, except for the architects who designed New Zyzzyzywa. They have obtained permission to continue to live and work in Old Zyzzyzywa. At the start of each morning I eat some natural breakfast food designed by my sister-in-law, who creates these experimental products for export at the Ministry of Traditional Foods and read the official newspaper and the official opposition newspaper. The editorials in both are written by the same team, using different pseudonyms. . . . As I drive into the old walled city along a highway whose smoothness and fine curves only my Mercedes can appreciate, I often pass the carpool of whores returning home after a long night. I wave at one Zzylstyra, with whom I once spent many lovely times in the pre-restoration downtown, when there were good cafés still open to locals that actually had refrigerated beer. Ah for those innocent days, when nobody cared about authenticity, when my uniform . . . ▌

▌85mar24 from clark humphrey
. . . when my uniform was a simple affair that a bachelor could iron in minutes. The old uniform was a symbol of honest oppressive authority. My people knew I was boss, but that I was really one of them with a boss above me. Now I have a beautiful, dignified appearance and a beautiful, dignified car, which serve to impress the internationals—but not to impress them with my power, only with the power of this hour's government. The locals know this, that I am now a mere entertainer, and their knowledge of this makes them more headstrong when I must enforce the law. . . . Only among the foreign community do I still get the thrill of being feared. (IN.S.OMNIA)▌

Restless Nights in the Electronic City: What Is IN.S.OMNIA?

"IN.S.OMNIA. Restless nights, an intense state of wakefulness. IN.S.OMNIA. Disquieting dreams, after curfew, in the conquered city." So begins the message that greets new users.

> **Interlingual intersections of the civic nervous system. People connected to one another by filaments of gregarious informativeness. A literary bulletin board system designed, in the words of Joyce, 'for the ideal reader with the ideal case of insomnia.' Welcome all callers pseudonymous, anonymous, or eponymous. (IN.S.OMNIA 1984)**

What is IN.S.OMNIA? That simple question requires a series of increasingly complex answers.

In one sense IN.S.OMNIA is simply an IBM PC clone sitting in the dark in Gyda's spare bedroom. The computer is connected to a single phone line. Callers, referred to as "users," use computers and modems to dial up the system, awaken it, and sign on under the name of their choice. The simple software sends out a few introductory texts (or "messages") that appear on the user's screen. Then a menu appears listing a number of topics or "rooms."

> **Lobby> That Night in Zyzzyzzzyzwa> Literary Sins> . . . dUMMY in WONDERLAND> Naive Writing> YUP SOAP> reporters at large> Derrida> HUGE STOREWIDE SALE> Faulkner> War of the Words> Rimbaud, Bad Blood Part 2>Whining about Orthography 101> Marginalia> Successful Singles> Me versus Myself> Tristram's Shanty (IN.S.OMNIA 1986)**

The user selects a room and gives a command to read the messages therein either FORWARD (in the chronological order of their entry) or in REVERSE (starting with the most recent).

▌85jan06 from Eugene Correct
Thank you. Now I am going to kill myself. BLAMMMMOOOO! There, I did it. I just
blew my brains out with a big gun. Now I'm dead. This is fascinating. A new
experience. No sounds at all. Otherwise, everything seems normal. Ah! . . . now
there's a ringing in my ears, no doubt because the gun made such a loud noise
when I shot myself. Isn't that funny? Just like real life. In a little while I'll clean
up the mess I made. I think, in the meantime, that I'll just watch MTV.▌

The room's messages flow steadily onto the user's screen until the user gives the command to STOP and GOTO the next room and scan the messages there. At any point the user may press E for ENTER and write a new message, which joins the others in that room.

▌85jan10 from Pienso Delgado
Hey, I'm a little upset. Why did this Eugene kill himself? Really? (IN.S.OMNIA)▌

But IN.S.OMNIA is more than this. It is a zone where certain familiar functions of reading and writing seem to occur, but in conditions that are completely new. What kind of writing is this that parades a glowing alphabet across a black screen? What kind of writing is this that is evanescent, that exists in front of you, then ceases to exist at the touch of a key?

▌84sep15 from Actual Size
. . . once you were content to simply eat your words. Now you have to inject them
with a needle. It's been three or four years since reading gave you any kind of a
rush at all.
You hate yourself. You're still not too far gone to wonder aghast at what you put
into your body last night. You shot up the good stuff weeks ago. The TV GUIDE
and the junk mail . . . where did that go?▌

What kind of writing is this in which text is recorded invisibly in one place—stored in electronic memory as a chain of ones and zeroes—but appears identically as alphanumeric characters in multiple, distant locations?

▌84sep15 from Actual Size
But . . . what words those were! Last night was good, you liked it a LOT. What
will those words do inside your body? (IN.S.OMNIA)▌

Users of IN.S.OMNIA quickly realize that here is a mechanics of writing that only travesties the culture of writing with ink and paper. This is writing on a new surface—a still, black lagoon in which glowing words float to the surface—that carries with it no immediate precedents, no protocols, no expectations.

Handwriters cultivate personal rituals of the favorite notebook, the special pen. Readers come to associate books of a certain size, a certain heft and smell with the pleasure they had reading them. Over time these habits and associations become institutionalized. These arbitrary qualities cease to be perceived as quirks and begin to be considered natural, inevitable, necessary—the essence of literacy. In.s.omniacs and other users of bulletin boards employ a culture of reading and writing outside of the book.

Bulletin board writing has its own start-up rituals; instead of the blank page, there is the dialing modem. Ringing. The bulletin board picks up and begins to hiss. Your machine shrieks in reply. The tones of the two machines lock in an information kiss. Across your screen come the words "WELCOME TO IN.S.OMNIA."

"To call long distance," writes in.s.omniac Dusty Miller, "to hear the warble of the data stream; the exultation as I realize that the miracle has happened, the phone is not busy, the board is not down (IN.S.OMNIA 1993). . . ."

The scratching of pen on paper is replaced by the clicking of keys and the response of the system at the other end of the line.

"I usually wrote late at night," in.s.omniac Frank Function writes of a period of ardent participation. "There was no other activity going on around me, usually not even the radio. . . . The softly pulsing cursor was a polite but impatient companion. Even when I got up to consult the dictionary I felt the cursor calling me back to the screen to continue. It was a constant reminder that only one user could log onto the system at a time and that others were waiting for me to finish (IN.S.OMNIA 1993)."

Just as the arbitrary length of papyrus scrolls divided ancient texts into "books," and the codex cut the flow of lines into pages, so screen dimensions create a new field for formal play. Clever in.s.omniacs quickly explore the technical possibilities, like early scribes putting a wax tablet through its paces. They begin using short line length to speed up the pace on the screen: narrow doggerel and doodles that race vertically. Others clear the screen entirely with black spacebars and create a night sky with a few starry asterisks. As a new user you quickly learn to make your own contributions, filling the memory buffer with careful keystrokes, then giving the triumphant order to SAVE onto the system.

85 m a r 1 9   f r o m   M u l t a t u l i
I would like to see a buffer that stores rhythms as well as text. Often the speed

- - - - - - - - - - - - - - -

and rhythm at which a message is typed is like speech inflection; pauses, racing ahead, backspaces, sometimes two can ad-lib off each other and it is almost like jazz. (IN.S.OMNIA)▌

In this world "scrolling" is as basic a phenomenon as the page turn is to the culture of books. On IN.S.OMNIA the term scrolling does not just refer to the steady disappearance of lines of text "off" the top of the screen as new lines flow in at the bottom. It also names a systemwide phenomenon. Because of a programmer's oversight (or stroke of brilliance), when the maximum number of messages the system can hold is reached, whole messages get erased, or "scrolled off the system." But the erasures are random, unrelated to the messages' ordering or age. This gives all messages a haunting, mortal quality that is most acute when the bulletin board is most active.

▌**8 5 f e b 2 4   f r o m   c r a n k y**
Eugene, I wonder how many interesting messages will scroll off into infinity because of your last message. Why don't you watch your ass, boy?▌

▌**8 5 f e b 2 4   f r o m   R i c o   E .   G u a p o**
How many interesting messages scrolled because of THAT message?▌

▌**8 5 f e b 2 4   f r o m   P i e n s o   D e l g a d o**
How many interesting messages scrolled because of THIS message?▌

▌**8 5 f e b 2 4   f r o m   T H A T   W I N S O M E   O T H E R**
How many messages have scrolled interestingly? (IN.S.OMNIA)▌

And over in the "Derrida Room" you find:

▌**8 5 f e b 1 8   f r o m   M u l t a t u l i**
Where's the first text? Scrolled into oblivion, friends. We are commenting on, and annotating, a quickly absent original. Truly no origins here. Beginning is always an interruption. (IN.S.OMNIA)▌

What is IN.S.OMNIA? An eerie discourse somewhere between speech and writing. The silent immediacy of the messages draws you in, night after night.

▌**8 5 f e b 0 1   f r o m   E u g e n e   C o r r e c t**
You probably all thought I was dead! Well, I am, but I'm having fun anyway. I'm up in the third level of the Bardo now, still working, but now I'm self-employed. I own Bardo Bill's Discount Used Cars and I'm making a killing. The business

practically runs itself, and I have lots of free time. So I've been going to movies,
and writing! Here's a story:
ECRITURE FROM THE BLACK LAGOON
Boats are fun, the water is mysterious, the prow cleaves the mother of us all. It
is your mother. Thalassa! It's very warm here, what's going to happen? . . .
(IN.S.OMNIA)▌

The darkness of the night, the darkness of the screen, and the liberation from
the pressures that school and work have conspired to place on your practices of writing make
this experience fresh, thrilling, intimate. You are like the refugee who has just escaped the
maelstrom and stands on some unknown high road, penniless, alone, but alive.

▌8 5 j u l 2 2   f r o m   O N E
One asks oneself how the others feel about having to use a question mark in
order to interrogate. One wonders if their hearts race, if their voices rise, if their
impatience boils at the end of a sentence. One wonders simply, declaratively.
One wonders while reclining on the sofa in the rented rooms one has occupied
since one can remember.
One has a choice to make. (IN.S.OMNIA)▌

The rediscovered passion of writing, the release from the restraint of old forms
and roles, is not an occurrence limited to small bulletin boards such as IN.S.OMNIA. It occurs
in the mighty electronic networks of business and academia as well. "Open, free-ranging
discourse has a dark side," say social scientists Lee Sproull and Sara Kiesler in an article in
Scientific American (1991).

The increased democracy associated with electronic interactions in our experiments interfered with decision making. . . . The results confirmed that the proportion of talk and influence of higher-status people decreased when group
members communicated by electronic mail.

The electronic format has not yet developed hierarchies. It acts as a sudden,
temporary equalizer. The crucial signs that surround spoken words (clothing, intonation,
body language) and texts (marketing, design, paper quality) are absent.

In literary terms, as in.s.omniac Paul Cabarga (letter 1992) comments: "The
status difference between reader and writer is effaced as they reverse roles. The reader does
not need the consent or cooperation of a third party to make a response public." *Invisible*

Seattle's Omnia (1986, 1) continues: "You are the audience, the auditor, the speaker, the reader, the writer—constantly shifting gears, enjoying all roles."

What results of this role effacement do Sproull and Kiesler see in their studies? "We also found that people tended to express extreme opinions and vented anger more openly in an electronic face-off than when they sat together and talked. Computer scientists using the ARPANET have called this behavior "flaming."

What is IN.S.OMNIA? A zone of spontaneous combustion, where users are invited to betray the smoldering world stifled beneath the conventions of writing and speech.

But the new user to IN.S.OMNIA rapidly sees that there is more going on here than a simple field day. There are investigations in progress, experiments in the strict sense: hypotheses being tested and evaluated.

How do in.s.omniacs describe their goals? The printed *Invisible Seattle's Omnia* (10) magazine of 1985 contains this formulation.

Let's dispense quickly with the human, all too human, motives of "getting into print." . . . the board is an experiment, a phenomenon with its own interest—an interest far surpassing most small magazines. Interesting not because we are better writers, etc., but because something about the board destroys many of the categories by which we deal with writing. . . . What we're saying to the reader is "come join us," "come explore with us," "come astonish us!" Don't just read or say this is good this is bad—write!

All texts here are equally out of place, from blurted confessions to stolen passages from the classics. This love of transgression of all kinds—hierarchical, stylistic—indicates a larger answer to the question what is IN.S.OMNIA?

IN.S.OMNIA is a workshop of transgression and juxtaposition. In a uniform style of presentation, drastically different texts follow one another as if it were the most natural thing in the world.

As often as not, the goal of the in.s.omniac who paces feverishly around her terminal in the dark of night—who ransacks shelves and memory for the ideal text to enter, oblivious of ownership or originality—is the search for maximum contrast. What will blow everybody away? What will be completely apt in this room, but completely unexpected. Something from the past, maybe. Something royal, austere, moralistic. Early Christian natterings. Something apocryphal or pseudepigraphal. In *Greek*! Transliterated Greek followed by a translation, a mistranslation!

"Please no literature with a capital L," began an early message that set a course for IN.S.OMNIA's more rigorous investigations. The call, instead, was for writing.

> . . . writing that is not trying to counterfeit any particular off-line genre or form. **WRITING THAT DOES NOT KNOW WHAT IT IS** but seeks, rather, to interrogate the world around it, the language within it and within which it takes place. In short, anything goes. Lies, hallucinations, shopping lists . . . foreplay, wordplay, logo-machy, abulia, echolalia, and most taboo of all in the real world, abstract intellectual conversation and scholarly meditation. (IN.S.OMNIA 1984)

An early paradigm of these team researches was the turbulent and problematic "Naive Writing Room." "This room continues a discussion started over a pleasant dinner but by no means finished," began its inaugural message.

> People speak of "Naive Painting" with all the ambiguous overtones of the word. "Naive" as in self-taught or academically untrained. Lacking knowledge of perspective, etc. "Naive" as in a strikingly different vision of the world —the other or the outsider. "Naive" as in uncalculated, innocent of any designs to create "ART" and so forth. . . . We begin to wonder, over dessert, whether we can speak of a "Naive Writing," and, if so, what is it?

> Grothus discovered a manuscript in a parking lot (what a title for a story, Ms. Found in a Parking Lot) . . . it was a series of pictures and texts—scrawled in impressively poor penmanship—like a fourth or fifth grader's . . . Abdellah Grillo (see the Derrida room) also belongs here. He is a limit case—supreme example of the URGE TO WRITE coupled with NO LITERARY AMBITIONS WHATSOEVER. He is driven to cover walls [of Fez, Morocco], trees, rocks, his clothes, books in libraries with an unreadable but evocative pseudo-writing. (*Invisible Seattle's Omnia* 1985, 10)

The exhibits entered in this room soon set a standard for juxtaposition that infected the rest of the bulletin board:

> **84jan09 from Grothus**
> — **Obtaining the Death Certificate**
> — **Conveyance from hospital or home**
> — **Embalming**
> — **Providing the correct raiment**
> — **Providing the casket**

Contact the man in the dark grey suit.
Barney Raymond Ltd.
121, D.S. Senanayake Mawatha, Colombo 8

Dear Bob, where do I begin? I'll just start by saying I care but don't love you.

BITE LIP if in trouble
Flip off Devil
left kingdom
heaven of hand
the Bible is one word God's name▌

▌85mar02 from Multatuli
In 1973, while in Santiago, immediately after the coup which overthrew Allende,
I found myself hypnotized by the daily newspapers. Only two were still allowed to
publish and, then, only on condition that they wrote about how wonderfully
everything was going, how happy the Chilean people were that the Armed Forces
had fulfilled its historic mission . . . all of this appearing daily during a period of
sheer terror. You can't imagine the THRILL of reading this stuff when you've just
come off a street with half-tracks, machine guns, and arbitrary searches.▌

▌85mar06 from Grothus
Shortest top for weight lifting
Swim suit
Buy books for Chem. & Phyc. [sic]
Mail income tax get state
get gas
get swimming locker
take uniform to work (this line crossed out in original sample)▌

▌85mar09 from Multatuli
I am trying to write differently—maybe I'm not trying—maybe I'm just dreaming
of writing differently—I feel somehow that my taste crystallized around certain
models that I unconsciously try to approximate or reproduce—certain rhythms,
sentence lengths, etc. . . . for this reason it's not idiotic to examine things that
aren't "writing as we know it" as a way of enlarging the boundaries of the possible. I'm convinced that if you read supermarket lists, censored newspapers, the
fine print on legal contracts, and GREAT LITERATURE, your writing will be more
interesting than if you just read GREAT LIT alone. (IN.S.OMNIA)▌

IN.S.OMNIA's capabilities for accommodating a media-age version of the art of
storytelling became clear in an explosion of texts that came to be known as *That Night in
Zyzzyzzzywa.* Over the years the in.s.omniacs' research into precedents of collaborative fiction

had identified a persistent quandary: the add-on story. Most collaborative fictions founder because of the linear structure of the conventional narrative. Writers pass the accumulating tale to one another, but only the first has true creative freedom. The subsequent writers are increasingly hemmed in, doomed to study the precedents to avoid continuity errors. One night on IN.S.OMNIA, in a modest little room devoted to word play, a simple message appeared.

85mar09 from Brent Olson
Define "zyzziva." Have fun.

After a few days of simple gags—"(E)va Gabor, dropped in a vat of 7-Up"; "a tropical weevil"—Arthur T. Murray proudly revealed that it was the town name that comes last on every list of American towns.

" . . . you and me still have a chance to change all that," the magnificent Sikuan replied that same night.

Of course the major problem is that we would have to found a town, but I am sure a very small one would suffice. From "Zyzziva" . . . we should keep the first four letters. But most definitely we must change the fifth from "i" to "y" . . . if some creep comes in and changes the seventh letter to any vowel . . . we can overcome that unfair dude by a trick played in many languages throughout the world, by reduplication of the root, so we could arrive at a "Zyzzyzzywa," but let's keep that up our sleeve.

Then . . .

85mar13 from Multatuli
"Zyzzyzzywa" . . . I've been there never having suspected that it was founded by Sik and Arthur T. So it was your equestrian statue I spied on the main plaza that late autumn afternoon . . .

85mar19 from Eugene Correct
THAT NIGHT IN ZYZZYZZZYWA
The only thing I'll remember about it was the harmonica, some droning harmonica, it never stopped—what was the tune—Stardust. I was suffocating on the honeysuckle, it was so hot the mosquitoes were taking the night off . . .

. . . and the community of Zyzzyzzzyzyzyzwa (the name was open to manipulation, getting progressively longer) was born.

▮85mar21 from Multatuli
That night in ZYZYZYZYZyzyzywa. I remember it well, better than you Eugene—I'd
just come in off the streets—three days of hiding from the government troops—
it was hot—you were right about that—but the music!—there wasn't any music—
music was banned in Zyzzyzzywa . . . ▮

So began the message that at one stroke solved the add-on story dilemma. By *contradicting* the previous message, by arguing facts and events, by throwing all the messages around it into doubt, the door was opened for anyone to join, to invent, to rhapsodize and not worry about continuity.

▮85mar21 from Mehitabel
Wow, you guys really brought back memories of Zyzzyzzywa. Of course, you two
couldn't be expected to remember too much, given the amount of drugs and alco-
hol you'd consumed by the time I got there. . . . (IN.S.OMNIA)▮

Why pretend that a story is written by one, when it is written by many? That was the lesson of Zyzzyzyzyzyzyzywa.

Zyzzyzyyzzzyzyyzyzywa was a boom town that expanded in a matter of weeks to have a history, a political scene, and a fleet of foreign "technical advisors." It also was quite clearly a cathartic working out of imperial guilt. This is what happened when Americans free-associated around a place name in 1985—their imaginations followed their tax dollars through covert pathways to the Third World.

What Zyzyzyzyzyyzzyyzyzyzyyzyzywa proved was that the tastes for juxtaposition and collaboration could coexist in the new electronic environment.

"Environment," a curious word to use for a catalog of texts. "Environment," "space," "zone," geographic terms such as these are consistently employed by users to describe the experience of an electronic bulletin board, whether or not it contains overtly geographic fictions like the ubiquitous "dungeons" or lands such as Zyzyzyzyzyzyzyzyzyzyzyzyzyyzyyzyzyzywa.

What is IN.S.OMNIA? It clearly feels like a "somewhere" not a "something." We are now beyond a simple exchange of literary texts and into the realm of the conceptual and experiential. IN.S.OMNIA, like telecommunication networks of all kinds, undermines our concept of unity of place. We are forced to reexamine childhood assumptions. You used to have to physically share a space with someone to conduct a dialogue. Now an easy form of dialogue can be performed with no regard to distance. The resulting violation of the old *distance-equals-the-time-needed-to-traverse-it* equation puts a corresponding crunch on the notion of time.

We all know these things. But do we have a vocabulary for them yet? Has our culture spent so much time spurning the industrial and now electronic revolutions (as too fast, too crass, too "mass") that it has yet to find names for, let alone understand, the phenomena we experience every day?

"Since the birth of the Minitel [the small computer terminal the French national phone system offers to every subscriber], a hundred small towns need to be added to the map of France," wrote Guy Sitbon in *Le Nouvel Observateur* in January of 1987.

These are the services where people gather on a regular basis. You're a "miniteller," you type a code, let's say NOEMIA. On NOEMIA you meet Brigitte, 27, a teacher, divorced, who lives in Brest. She likes travel and gardening. She tells you things about the breakup of her marriage she's never told anyone. You meet Patrick, 48, an engineer from St. Etienne. He tells you to take what Brigitte says with a grain of salt. She was never really married to the father of her child.

Noemia is a village where everyone knows each other. In it we are all better looking, more intelligent. We show ourselves as we would like to be, and it does us good. When I've had enough of living in Noemia, I take a trip. All I need to do is touch the CONNECT button . . . and I am teleported in the wink of an eye to another town, where I join Jacques, Eric, Odile, other friends, other dreams.

What is IN.S.OMNIA? Some futuristic high-tech replacement for physical functions that have become too slow? A slick, faddish, real-time virtual universe that allows its users to run free in some utopian Salem colony of heightened consciousness? Well . . . not until some in.s.omniac wins that big lottery grand prize and spends a zillion on software, it isn't!

No, IN.S.OMNIA is a simple little machine with a clunky program that blows its gasket and goes off-line from time to time. And its projects aren't necessarily all done on the system. A full technical description of IN.S.OMNIA must include the phone calls and letters exchanged by those users who know each other off-line as they fan the flames of a particular room, a particular project. IN.S.OMNIA is a part-time passion of a handful of people—

demographically skewed toward those wealthy enough to afford a computer and modem (further skewed in the early days by the maleness and whiteness of 1980s computer usage)— whose use of the bulletin board vacillates with time and interest.

But IN.S.OMNIA exists whether the computer is up or down, whether or not a project is under way. More than software and hardware, IN.S.OMNIA is a habit of association, a set of behaviors of creation, behaviors that users remember long after they have signed off the board. From their voyages in the microcosm of IN.S.OMNIA in.s.omniacs emerge armed with a paradigm that allows them to see some of the workings of the greater world of telecommunications.

The admirable Myron Krueger, in his book *Artificial Reality* (1991, 17), shows an interesting pair of diagrams. He calls it the Videoplace Concept and distinguishes between "telecommunications":

and his own term "artificial reality":

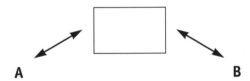

In.s.omniacs ask: Why not dispense with the double-headed arrow entirely? Don't theorists tell us that all communication involves the pretense of moving persons A and B onto an artificial common ground—say, a language—where they struggle and play?

The lesson of network communities such as IN.S.OMNIA is that they become extensions of—not alternatives to—our everyday communities. They allow us to live in two places at once (minimum: two worlds). They force us to realize that we behave differently under new constraints, become different people at different times (minimum: two selves). They show us that—through combinations of media, memory, and imagination—geographic zones are already constantly interpenetrating.

What is IN.S.OMNIA? Finally, perhaps, a structural, *geographic* model of the workings of language itself.

The pleasure of language, some would say, lies in the ways it fails to work, the way it constantly implies the existence of direct, straight-line communication, but in fact always transports interlocutors to an artificial playing field on which they enact ritualized encounters. There is a long history of disparagement of mediated communications (pen-and-paper writing chief among them) on the basis of their substitute status in comparison to physical presence. IN.S.OMNIA urges us to think of its playing field, its geography, as just another path in the everyday world.

For example, if one includes the phone calls that are often a part of an active writing project on IN.S.OMNIA, the structure of the event could be diagrammed like this:

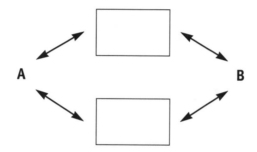

This *circuit* seems to correspond more accurately to the ways in which we use telecommunications on a daily basis: two people talking on the phone while watching the same TV broadcast, for example.

IN.S.OMNIA encourages us to use these "circuit diagrams," these maps, as analogies for thinking about writing and other media in the "information age," rather than the supposed straight line from author to reader.

The geographic strand in the in.s.omniacs' thinking predates IN.S.OMNIA. It is rooted in the misty and ancient history of Invisible Seattle.

exempli gratia iii

This occurred during the "period of the phone calls." Every time we started to dial a number, we intersected other lines. Conversations of such appalling banality we were convinced they were staged. Summaries of television shows just seen, new therapies, diets, etc. Desperate, we contacted a newspaper (you know it well, reader, permit me to omit its name—all proper nouns are interchangeable in INVISIBLE SEATTLE), and we attempted to place the following ad:

WANTED: vaulting ambition, social upheaval, tumult in the council chambers, a more resonant history.

WANTED: crowds at night, live music in elevators, boulevards to channel our dreams, cafés to house our passionate wranglings.

WANTED: ambience, shadow, majesty. (Wohlstetter 1980)

You won't see me at

INVISIBLE SEATTLE

INVISIBLE SEATTLE
MASTER USE PERMIT APPLICATION

Dear Master User:

This is your official INVISIBLE SEATTLE Master Use Permit Application Form, #864★, designed for use in the 1881-1982 fiscal century. Forms should be completed in triplicate, typed, written legibly, or written in an imitation of Sophie Tauber's handwriting and illuminated with gold leaf. Illustrations, charts, maps, diagrams, xerograms, anagrams, grandmagrams etc. can be included, but must be severely labeled. Absolutely all accompanying visual materials should be good. Any applications containing restraint, reasonable alternatives, compromises, brass tacks, concessions to the private sector, or bottom lines will be dismissed out of hand. If you cheat on this application, you're only cheating yourself. Practical limitations: None. This is mandatory. Permits will be awarded on the basis of pith and merit. Applications should be postmarked no later than August 18th, to 1822 - 17th Ave., Seattle WA 98122. Consideration of Master Use Permit Applications will take place September 6, 1982, in the Alki Room (Caffe Starbucks) of the Seattle Center, at 3:45 p.m., at a Public Hearing before the Court of Miracles of INVISIBLE SEATTLE. Do not start filling out your application until I say the word: "Begin." "Glad you could make it. We've been waiting for you.

Begin,

Bobo

NAME_____ DATE_____ Pick you up at ☐8:00 ☐8:30 ☐9:00

What Your Friends Call You_____ PREFERRED AGE_____

FAVORITE ARCHITECT_____ RANDOM NUMBER_____

FAVORITE WATERING HOLE_____

SITE:

Location:_____ Color _____

Size of Lot_____

Present owner_____ Future owner, if any_____

Latitude _____ Longitude _____

Pulcritude _____ Platitude"_____"

Best Time of Day to View the Site_____

Any Existing Structures?_____If so, Brief Description;_____
_____

PROPOSAL

Alteration of Existing Structure

☐Addition of Ears
☐Addition of Feet
☐Addition of Wings
☐90° Rotation
☐180° Rotation
☐Inversion
☐Camouflage (specify)
☐Other (Please describe in detail, using the back of this sheet for verbal representations, and the space provided below for pictorial representations.)

New Structure

If your New Structure is to be built on the site of an existing structure, do you want the existing structure to be:
☐Forgotten
☐Torn Down Stone by Stone, by an Angry Mob
☐Shrunk, and Placed in the Museum of the Folly of Man
☐Left to Co-exist With Your Structure
☐Reconstructed Elsewhere as an Object Lesson. Where? _____

Please describe your project in detail, using the back of this sheet for verbal representations, and the space provided below for pictorial representations.

Architect's Musing

On the back of this sheet, write the first three sentences of a short story set in your new, or altered structure. No application will be considered complete without this.

How long has this idea been incubating in your mind?_____   If accepted, in whose name is your project to be dedicated? __
_____   _____

Where were you when this idea first occured to you?_____   Where did you obtain this application?_____
_____   _____

To whom did you first confide your idea?_____   How long have you lived in Invisible Seattle?_____

Invisible Seattle flyers joined the thriving cacophony of early '80s telephone pole art.

Since 1979 Invisible Seattle has conspired to "take over the city by hypnotic suggestion." Each of our acts has been an attempt to inject an element of "fiction" into the so-called "reality" of an unsuspecting average American metropolis and self-proclaimed livable city.

Proper and improper authorities immediately accused us of trying to induce a collective hallucination. In fact, we have been trying to free ourselves and others from an imposed collective hallucination: "the city of skyscrapers donuts and boredom." That city (your city) has already been conquered by towers of glass and steel saying to all who stare up helplessly at them: obey, adore, be silent. That city and all of its structures are "found objects," not created by you or me, but capable of being RE-created. Borrowing as a weapon the Surrealist notion of "changing the destination of an object," Invisible Seattle assigns names, and thus, meanings to structures built by developers and hustlers in order to remap and repossess this conquered city. If the slogan of the modern movement is "Form Follows Function," Invisible Seattle's is "Function Follows Fiction." (*Invisible Seattle's Omnia* 1985, 87)

Hi, I'm Ivan. Why bomb me?

(I've got this great date lined up with Tanya down in the Maintenance Office.)

DON'T BE UNAVAILABLE FOR COMMENT!
Come meet Ivan, Gedla, Pajni, Sven, Rossetta, Claube, Ahmep, Beddleti, Juliana, Mimi, Smith, Smith and all their friends as

INV SBLE S ATTLE
INVISIBLE SEATTLE
INVISIBLE SEATTLE

scales the Bobo Memorial Omnilateral Summit
to discuss Options, Captions, Raptures, Ramifications, Overtakes,
Underlooks, Reactive Protection, Protective Reaction, Overtakes,
Protracted Rejection, Active Roentgens, Policy Splits, Projected Retraction
Manoeuvres, Undervention, Inspiration, Downheaval, Painless Tripartisan
Reckless Optimisim, Comprehensive Frameworks, Cautious Pessimism,
Impacted Wisdom, Uptrodden Majorities, Reflation, Incession, Derision,
Repletion, Spotty Attendance, Infirm Resolve, Overdue Speed, Descalations,
Re-elevations, hikes, dips, slides, surges and hugs in preparation to visibilize
at Bumbershoot '81.

Welcome all Artists, Poets, Actors, Dancers, Architects, Idle Men, Fallen Women, All Persons of
Slender Means, Dubious Antecedents, and Questionable Loyalties!

TIME: 8:00-10:00 p.m.
DATES: Aug 3, 10, 17
PLACE: Elliott Bay Cafe
Your visa will be validated at
the long table in back.

Jules Verne

Astonish Me.

Pioneer Square

Promenade in the Bois de Balloon

Aurora Bridgralis

At The Court of Miracles

TERRA INCOGNITA

Nadja

1	Bobo's Head	21	Garden of Eden
2	Valparaiso	22	Bogue Plaza
3	The Communicating Vessels	23	Temple of Venus
4	The Waldorf Hysteria	24	Moulin Rouge
5	Alaska Exposition	25	The Washington Pizza
6	Lake Celine	26	The Joe Diamond Desert
7	Mont San Michel Winery	27	War of the Worlds Park
8	Bored More	28	The Bauhaus Restaurant
9	Pope's Summer Residence	29	Capitalist Hill
10	Big House	30	Muttering Heights
11	St. Marks		
12	Les Champs Magnetiques		
13	El Reloj Caido en el Mar		
14	The Daily Planet		
15	Needle of Space		
16	The Harry Lime Ferris Wheel		
17	The Court of Miracles		
18	Van Gogh Memorial		
19	Off the Wall Playhouse		
20	Chief Seattle		

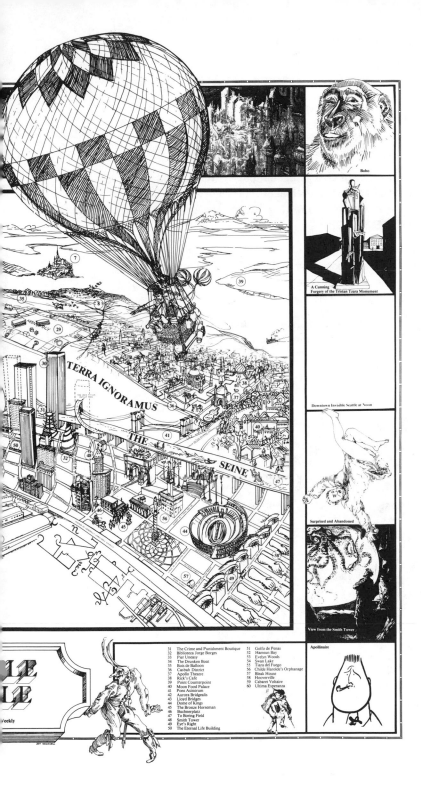

TERRA IGNORAMUS

THE SEINE

Bobo

A Cunning
Forgery of the Tristan Tzara Monument

Downtown Invisible Seattle at Noon

Surprised and Abandoned

View from the Smith Tower

Apollinaire

31 The Crime and Punishment Boutique	51 Golfo de Penas
32 Biblioteca Jorge Borges	52 Hamsun Bay
33 Pier Uneasy	53 Evelyn Woods
34 The Drunken Boat	54 Swan Lake
35 Bois de Balloon	55 Tiara del Fuego
36 Casbah District	56 Childe Harolde's Orphanage
37 Apollo Theatre	57 Bleak House
38 Rick's Cafe	58 Hooverville
39 Point Counterpoint	59 Cabaret Voltaire
40 Moon Food Palace	60 Ultima Esperanza
41 Poms Asinorum	
42 Aurora Bridgealis	
43 Lloyd Bridges	
44 Dome of Kings	
45 The Bronze Horseman	
46 Buchnerplatz	
47 To Boring Field	
48 Smith Tower	
49 Eye's Right	
50 The Eternal Life Building	

1980 Program of Events [selected events]
Monday, September 1

3:30 Academy of Not-American Poets; Reading of Pushkin, Baudelaire, Icelandic, and old English poets in the original languages

4:30 Scenes from the History of Invisible Seattle. A tableau of our rich history of French revolutions, subtle heresies, and artistic deviations. History invented before your eyes by the Off The Wall Players

5:00 Trials of the Enemies of Civic Life. Poet prosecutors to deliver impassioned phillipics against the yahoo of their choice. Qualifications: Shameless greed, arrogant stupidity. The audience as jury. The guilty to be declared COMPLETELY VISIBLE. Music by Czigany.

7:15 Beyond the Call of Beauty. The ultimate beauty contest. The contestants are verbal descriptions of perfect beauty read aloud by actors. The judges and audience imagine them (to musical accompaniment) and grade them 1 to 10. With Czigany.

PLUS, Artbucks auction, Invisible Seattle Museum, and the intermittent showing of Elvis Presley's "It Happened at the World's Fair." (Invisible Seattle 1980b)

Preliminary Oneiric survey has confirmed the existence of three major zones of INVISIBLE SEATTLE: the Ignored, the Imperceptible, and the Impossible.

Many districts in Seattle have lapsed into invisibility, ignored by speculators, unvisited by commerce. Time slowly accumulates its surprises until one day a street or avenue exerts an undeniable spell on the walker who has taken a wrong turn, who stands amazed, troubled, silent. To discover such a place in which the city that is to come announces its arrival takes more than eyesight. Others, surely, have admired the magnificent shadows of Western Avenue, that zone of warehouses and unexpected stairways, but to INVISIBLE SEATTLE belongs the honor of the first systematic verbal exploration. . . .

INVISIBLE SEATTLE, or the Imperceptible; the wider world whose presence betrays itself in any of a thousand ways. Inhabitant of Visible Seattle, you who drink Colombian coffee, wear Hong Kong shirts, switch on a Japanese TV set, sport Italian shoes and a Swiss watch, drive to work in a Volkswagen powered by Arab oil, you dance to invisible strings. INVISIBLE SEATTLE is the antidote to your feeling of completeness, to the illusion that the world ends at the city limits. Ah, Robinson, Robinson Crusoe! Beware of the invisible laws of economics. Beware of the invisible power of ideas. Every time you read a book you enter INVISIBLE SEATTLE.

INVISIBLE SEATTLE or the Call of the Impossible, the hallucination of a counterhistory and geography that we insist you share and revise, a region we simultaneously invent and defend with our lives. To arrive there at six o'clock on a summer evening is to encounter all the cities you've ever visited, snapshots of Cairo, faded newsreels, engravings of fog swirling around lampposts, maps full of blanks and question marks, erector sets, alleys glimpsed from the freeway as you're hitching through town, palm trees, headless statues, businesses you would have started if you had the money, languages you meant to learn, dreams forgotten instantly upon awakening, plazas where every evening a lover awaits you with open arms or a firing squad offers you a cigarette, a blindfold, and no explanation. (Wohlstetter 1981a)

"As great as New York and Paris are, . . . we cannot superimpose their personalities upon Seattle without arriving at an imitation so cheap and false it will shame the snows down off Rainier."

—Tom Robbins

"As great as New York and Paris are, . . . we cannot superimpose their personalities upon Seattle without arriving at INVISIBLE SEATTLE."

—Bobo

By direct satellite hookup from France, Poland, Czechoslovakia, Argentina, INVISIBLE SEATTLE has received the following response to your recent *Weekly* article: AMERICA HAS NOT DOMINATED THE ARTS SINCE WWII STOP TOM ROBBINS PREACHING CULTURAL REAGANISM STOP . . .

What—will you defend a city within whose boundaries you choose not to reside? Will you assign it a fixed identity ("relaxed radicalism") and protect it from foreign contamination?

Come, you amaze us! You have spread such nonsense, and we must ask you to publicly retract it—a disclaimer in the *Weekly* will do the trick. If you refuse the Court of Miracles of INVISIBLE SEATTLE sends you the following challenge: Appear, if you wish, at BUMBERSHOOT '81 in the Alki Room, Seattle Center grounds, Monday, September 7 at 5:00 p.m. Choose your weapons, your arguments, your seconds. . . . We offer you an exhilarating fight, a travesty of justice, a chance to defend yourself before an irrational and outrageously biased court of "aggressive and arrogant poseurs" to borrow a phrase of yours. (*Invisible Seattle* 1981)

Photos: Mark Wade

The judge and singing jury of the "outrageously biased court" assembled for Invisible Seattle's Trial of Tom Robbins in 1981. The raucous event took the northwest novelist to task for an article in which he defended the rustic purity of Seattle from pernicious foreign influence. Using the legalistic skit format, the invisibles poked manic fun at recieved ideas of the urban and the rural, depraved cosmopolitanism vs. "natural" agrarian morality.

International members of the Invisible Seattle foreign legion protest Robbins's assertion of an American-dominated world culture.

Even Robbins Gets the Blues

Author stuck in his own social slick, 'court' says

By Diane Wright

Herald Arts Writer

SEATTLE—Author Tom Robbins was tried last night.

Judging from the standing room only crowd in the Seattle Center Alki Room—renamed Caffe Starbuck's for Bumbershoot—half of Seattle was there to watch.

They'd been drawn to this literary kangaroo court by the prospect that

- - - - - - - - - - - - - -
38 ➡

Mark Wade

their favorite chronicler of pop culture would be among them. Earlier, he'd vowed to show up, but in disguise. If he did appear, he came and went like the legendary Masked Man—anonymously.

Robbins was charged with "cultural Reaganism" in response to an article he wrote called "The Cult of the Rude Meets the City of the Nice." In the article, Robbins slammed an influx of rude urbanites into Seattle—Mercedes cars, Gucci clothes, and Broadway hangouts. He referred to them with such juicy phrases as: "They (the Manhattan transfers and Beverly Hills rejects) are coach-class jet setters who simply couldn't make it in the faster lane of New York and Westwood." He advocated that "the Cult of the Rude should be regarded as a kind of social oil spill. Perhaps we should organize a Greenpeace unit to mop up Perrier pollution and to teach those responsible some manners."

Them's fighting words, and a group of ex-urbanites called Invisible Seattle got plenty riled over this. They proceeded to challenge Robbins to a "trial by his aesthetic peers."

With the help of a comedy group called the Off the Wall Players, they managed to stage a "Happening" that contained all the elements of Divorce Court, Let's Make a Deal, Saturday Night Live, Dean Martin's Celebrity Roast, and Soul Train.

Seattle's resident story-teller, Pleasant D. Spain primed the audience with a reading of the essay in question, to the varied accompaniment of hisses and applause.

Coby Scheldt and Joe Guppy of the Off the Wall Players then moved in with mikes for some live play-by-play action "Here from the Court of Miracles courtesy the Invisible Broadcast Service. . . ."

The court-appointed defense attorney pleads for clemency.

As court stenographer Andrea Stein (wearing white harlequin glasses) recorded the proceedings, other witnesses were trotted out. A genuine French person gave testimony as Judge Winchell laboriously tried to translate: "Monsieur Le Défenseur, parlez, examinez-vous." A brigade of the Invisible Seattle Foreign Legion, led by David Klein ("Badges,? We don't need no stinking badges.") burst in, a group that included one Brazilian, a Spaniard, and a Pole, arriving to refute Robbins's claim that "the U.S.A. has overwhelmingly dominated the arts since the end of World War II."

To puncture Robbins's assertion that the Cult of the Rude does nothing but hang out eating Gucci burgers in fern bars, the group called on Carl Gardner of KZAM-FM who had earlier gone on an investigative foray to capture live comments on tape from those selfsame fern bars. An over-whelming number of those interviewed were themselves Robbins read-ers. When asked why they read him, comments ran to: "I like the way his metaphors roll."

After a one-minute recess, in which the court played ball and made ketchup, mustard, and lettuce sandwiches out of Robbins's latest paperback, the proceedings got under way again. Paul Dorpat, an emissary of Robbins, presented four exhibits on his behalf, including a tenegeric by Pauline Kael, a discourse on electrons by J. Robert Oppenheimer, and Robbins's standard "I have caught my head in a mangle . . . I am indisposed for eternity" form letter. . . .

After remarkable heats of oratory in the summing up, in which the prosecution begged "Come back to Invisible Seattle, Tom, which you enter every time you jaywalk, where American Express never gets to know you, where there's valet [sic, actually: "ballet"] parking in front of every cafeteria," the Reverend Chumleigh used an ancient religious test to determine Robbins's guilt or innocence. Prefacing it with "Aren't you being kind of hard on the guy? I think it's nice when someone that age discovers free love," he dropped a paperback copy of "Another Roadside Attraction" in a small vat of water. If it floated, Robbins was innocent.

It sunk.

Guilty as charged.

As punishment, Robbins was declared Completely Visible. It was the end of two hours of sheer lunacy, one of the most memorable of Bumbershoot's many great moments. Too bad he had to be tried in absentia.

Tom, you missed a great party. (Wright 1981)

The chief prosecutor completes closing arguments.

Mark Wade

This Region We Invent and Defend: Mapping the Invisible

"The time has come to rescue our city from the ravages of nature. To erase the urban skyline and repaint it in our own invisible image."

A pickup truck full of windblown writers, artists, and performers pulls up beneath the downtown terminus of Seattle's monorail. It is Labor Day weekend of 1980. At the center of attention is the *Map of Invisible Seattle* (Invisible Seattle 1980c), hot off the press. The booming proclamation continues.

> **The time has come to rename downtown streets in hopes we all get lost. To try the enemies of civic life and declare them completely visible. To rediscover the traces of that Invisible Seattle whose implacably just laws rule our dreaming hours. Act quickly, citizens, or the game is lost. (cited in Wohlstetter and Wittig 1984)**

In a flourish, the monorail is officially rechristened "The Disorient Express." A copy of the *Map of Invisible Seattle* is presented ceremoniously to the deputy mayor.

With this typical Invisible event we embark on a flashback to the dawn of the Reagan era. It will take us along a trajectory of ideas through a series of publications and events that finally settled in the electronic community of IN.S.OMNIA.

In 1979, Philip Wohlstetter, along with James Winchell, Jean Sherrard, and Larry Stone, had extrapolated the title of Italo Calvino's marvelous suite of geo-imaginative accounts, *Invisible Cities*, into a collective pseudonym that signaled their intention to reimagine their surroundings. What interested them was the power of words and images to alter the way we experience geography. In selecting a city, "the city," as their central metaphor, they already were distancing themselves from the deep American Rousseauist tradition of countryside as the source of harmony, inspiration, and virtue—a tradition especially strong west of the Mississippi. Instead, they posited something resolutely artificial, cultural, historical. Instead of joining the long American search for simplicity, they opened their eyes and minds to complexity, to the invisible city of the ignored, the imperceptible, and the impossible.

The infrastructure of Invisible Seattle was not mysterious. Wohlstetter had been a member of the theatre troupe that now produced Seattle's yearly Bumbershoot arts festival. The festival provided the "invisibles," as they were called, with a venue for their performances. Eight pages from the center of Bumbershoot's Literary Arts *Schedule of Events* became the group's yearly tabloid, *The Daily Zeitgeist*.

The *Map of Invisible Seattle* is the central document of those early years; it contains the main boulevards of Invisible thought.

First, the fundamental gesture of proclaiming the *Map* official signals the group's usurpation of city government, claiming the roles of mayor, judge, and cartographer.

Then the *Map* bristles with architectural visitors. The Coliseum of Rome replaces the gray Kingdome stadium. Breughel's tower of Babel (labeled "Biblioteca Jorge Borges") replaces an office tower. Even the Space Needle, visible Seattle's most recognizable cliché, is replaced by the Eiffel Tower, the structure it clearly quotes.

The *Map* acknowledges that long before the age of electronic telecommunications cities represented a collapse of space. Cosmopolitan—the word suggests a community of foreigners who, by virtue of their memories and continued contacts with their homelands, turn a given city into a microcosm of the world. To show the Tower of Pisa leaning comfortably in the Denny Regrade is a challenge to the notion of unity of place, to the notion that Concord is Concord and Caracas is Caracas and never Mark Twain shall meet you there.

Likewise, the *Map* demonstrates the collapse of time implicit in cities. Every city is a museum of building styles, of booms and busts, of developers' dreams and military architects' obsessions. (Instead of ramparts, American cities are split by the interstate highway system, built as the Pentagon's private roadway, easily sealed off in case of war.)

The *Map* makes visible some of this lost history. For example, there is a drawing of Seattle architect Vergil Bogue's never-constructed dream. "That a man in 1910 could have chosen 4th and Blanchard as the site of a magnificent plaza," wrote Wohlstetter

(1980) in the *The Daily Zeitgeist*, "a dynamic hub of radiating avenues in the style of St. Peter's square or L'Enfant's Washington, D.C., seems incredible when we consider what is there now." In 1980 the neighborhood was neglected.

On the site of the current University of Washington, the *Map* shows a vanished fairground. "Why look in the jungle for lost cities when traces of them lie all around you in INVISIBLE SEATTLE?" the *Zeitgeist* article continues.

> **Such a city is the Alaska-Yukon-Pacific exposition of 1909. . . . Stranger than even Machu Picchu or Angkor Wat are these vanished cities of the last century—great expositions—palaces of steel and papier-mâché that arose suddenly in the heart of Paris, Chicago, Seattle, and just as suddenly vanished. What must we think then of these Disneylands in which Spain is represented by dancers fandangoing in a reconstructed Alhambra and Switzerland by Tyrolean-hatted peasants serving milk and cheese beside a cardboard mockup of the Alps? Not merely civic boosterism or the urge to amuse. An admirable desire lies behind all this—the desire to become the whole world. Within a city would appear another city—or rather all cities, all times, and all places. And so with INVISIBLE SEATTLE. We are an exposition that never closes and we, too, aspire to become the whole world. Here in Seattle, forty centuries of history look down upon us and the invisible stalks us at every street corner. (Wohlstetter 1980)**

Minimum: two eras at once.

In creating the *Map*, the invisibles were inscribing themselves in a long tradition of geographic imaginers—map makers, place namers, writers of letters home. The story of geographic disinformation in the Western hemisphere is long. Exiled to an ice-covered rock in the middle of nowhere, Eric the Red conspired to have the place called "Greenland" to attract some company. "Bella Vista." "Happy Valley." How are the streets of America paved? They are paved with the word "gold."

"Who describes America now?" the invisibles asked. Too often that task is left to those who understand their interest in it: developers, merchants, politicians. How many subdivisions, as Clark Humphrey has pointed out, are named after the geographical landmarks that were destroyed to build them? What was going on under this theme park of cheerful names? What the invisibles saw were cities full of Robinson Crusoes playing parts in a frontier mythology that did not include civic life. The myth of free lives in virgin spaces was acting as a substitute for history.

Conventional literary forms seemed only to perpetuate and at the same time conceal this myth—asserting that a masculinity-based, explorer/hero, "coming of age" narrative was universal and inevitable. The invisibles asked: What forms of language and line could reveal this myth and prepare it to be abandoned?

First, they decided, there must be a questioning of the Romantic division of writing into fiction and nonfiction. The three sacred genres—poem, story, novel—had come to claim subjectivity and the imagination as their own. Other forms that had been open to the "creative" writer through the end of the 18th century—bestiaries, handbooks for princes, meditations, hagiographies, etymologies, travel guides—were spurned as utilitarian, industrial, "objective." At best this world of other forms had been, as Russian critic Mikhail Bakhtin later asserted, subsumed into the novel and made to dance to the novel's tune. Poetry and fiction were held to embody a higher truth than their objective counterparts.

But a lot had happened to truth since the beginning of the 19th century. The truth claims of the Enlightenment, embodied in those "objective," encyclopedic forms, had eroded. By the late '60s it was common wisdom among literary theorists that no text could be a neutral text, that choices of inclusion, exclusion, and arrangement constantly betrayed—in fact trumpeted—the writer's passions and blind spots. The personality of the writer was held to be as evident in a biology paper as in a poem. The argument that a higher truth was to be found in conventional poetry and fiction alone was no longer tenable.

The form of the map itself became a paradigm for the invisibles of all the underutilized, underfictionalized forms waiting out there for creative writers to work with. The qualities of a map encouraged the invisibles to look beyond simple running text. A map is indissolubly visual and verbal. It is a data base from which different selections are made for different uses. It is interactive and random access. It is nonnarrative, although narratives may occur within it.

Second, the invisibles found specific encouragement in certain unclassifiable, creative, but definitely nonfictional texts such as the Surrealists' various searches for the marvelous in drab neighborhoods, the Situationists' psychogeography of Les Halles, and above all the methodical micro-recordings of the contemporary French writer Georges Perec.

Perec (1936–1982), once classified his protean writings into four different fields of investigation, four cardinal directions: the sociological, the autobiographical, the playful (formal games and experiments), and the novelistic. Because of the intertwining of these four directions in all his work—books such as *Things. A Story of the Sixties* (1990); *Penser/Classer* (*To Think/To Classify*) (1985); radio pieces such as "Tentative de description de choses vues au carrefour Mabillon le 19 mai 1978" ("An Attempt at a Description of Things Seen at Mabillon Junction on 19 May 1978"); and the mega-novel *Life A User's Manual*—Perec is a constant source of encouragement to the invisibles.

In a series of sociological inquiries called *Espèces d'Espaces* (*Species of Spaces*) (1984), Perec asked a question of startling simplicity: How does one look at the everyday world? "The problem is not to invent space," he writes, "much less to re-invent it (there are too many well-meaning people around already who make it their business to cogitate on our surroundings . . .) but to examine it, or, more simply, to read it; because what we call the everyday is not obvious, it is opaque: a kind of blindness, a type of anesthesia."

The Invisible Seattle truck that careened around the city renaming streets according to the new map ("I dub thee Aphrodisiastrasse, I dub thee Lysistrasse, I dub thee Street of the Men Who Walk Like Sinbad, Bleak Street, Bleaker Street, Bleakest Street") was attempting to counteract this anesthesia.

Realizing the work there was to be done in the realm of imaginative geography, it was hard for the invisibles not to feel disappointed with the insistence of the American literary machine on cranking out the same 200 novels every year. It was hard not to feel that fiction writers were at least missing a great opportunity, if not abdicating a responsibility. It was into this charged atmosphere, the next year, that unsuspecting novelist Tom Robbins sauntered with an article in a May, 1981 issue of Seattle's *Weekly*.

By the time the invisibles carefully planted the following interview in September, gallons of newspaper ink had already been spilt over the Robbins Affair.

Q: You're referring now to Tom Robbins's article in the *Weekly*, "The Cult of the Rude Meets the City of the Nice." What was your reaction to that article when it appeared?

A: Hives.

Q: Robbins seems to think that the slick young professionals in the Broadway bars are part of a cult of the rude inspired by European and particularly French culture.

A: That's true. He only "seems" to think. Thought would indicate that the

inspiration for the new wave of conspicuous consumption is Hollywood or Madison Avenue rather than the Left Bank. (Humphries 1981)

Robbins's article had run in early May, replying to an April article criticizing Seattle for being "too nice." The thrust of Robbins's text was simple and accurate: a distant early warning about the yuppie mannerisms that were to become hallmarks of the '80s. But Robbins piled on the barbs. They culminated in the assertion that ". . . the U.S.A. has overwhelmingly dominated the arts since the end of World War II." The invisibles issued a challenge, threatening a spectacular trial unless there was a retraction. The press took up the story. Robbins sparred graciously with the invisibles in a public exchange of interviews and articles throughout the month of August. No retraction was given.

On September 7, the day of the trial, Bumbershoot's sweltering coffeehouse was packed. Drawn by the publicity, spectators perched on window sills, handrails, and peered in through the windows.

Judge James Winchell made his musical entrance as a whip-cracking, pistol-packing embodiment of justice. "Let's get one thing straight!" he began. "This court is not about to be influenced by facts."

Any urchin above the age of seven can weigh evidence, ponder principles, and come to a considered decision. We're interested in unfounded opinion, anonymous rumor, ignorant sources from the center of ambition, and keyhole hearsay! We're not trying Robbins the man. By the way Tom, you've been wonderfully combative. And we're not trying his books—*Another Roadside Fatality*, *Even Cowgirls Read the News*, *My Still Life with a Woodpecker*. We're trying a cultural phenomenon to which the name of Tom Robbins has attached itself in the form of an article in the *Weekly*. (manuscript 1991)

A singing jury in choir robes, jumpropes at "recess," a roaming pair of narrator/reporters, unrehearsed testimony from the audience—the trial unfolded like a circus.

"Come back to the city, Tom," was the refrain of the Chief Prosecutor's closing argument.

Come back to the constant pressure of other minds that will sharpen your own ideas. Too long you have denied us your presence, your sheer gall, your love of language. You have persisted in your obstinate exile, living in the solitude of adulation, living Crusoe-like on your island of false simplicity and writing

articles that insist too much on why you like living where you live. Throw off the cowboy boots and come back into the rich confusion of city life. Either the killer condos and the fern bars will eat up the rest of the municipality or together we will defend our civic space and create the Invisible Seattle whose possibilities we can dimly sense. (Wohlstetter 1981b)

The next year's Invisible Seattle event was a city council meeting that extravagantly rejected the new city nickname authorized by the Chamber of Commerce and reviewed grant proposals and building permit applications, again to a packed house. The new element for the year was the application forms themselves: questionnaires that had been circulated and collected in the month preceding the event. This marked the first concerted attempt to solicit written input for a project. During the carnival atmosphere of the trials and hearings, collaboration had entered the mix of invisible ideas.

After three years of events, the invisibles were ready to combine geographic investigation, the search for new forms of writing, and collaboration in an ambitious new project.

exempli gratia iv

Rules of the Game

1. Find a city that needs a novel.

2. Delimit the city clearly with white chalk lines 2 inches in width. Events that occur on or within the chalked boundaries are considered "fair" for purposes of the novel, and may be included.

3. Rent a literary computer, or have a fabulous monster cyber-no-ziggurat built for your use. (The latter is highly recommended by the Rules Committee.)

4. The Object of the Game is to tickle a city into writing a great novel about itself in four seven-day periods of regulation time with an optional five-day overtime period in case of blockage. . . .

(Wittig 1983)

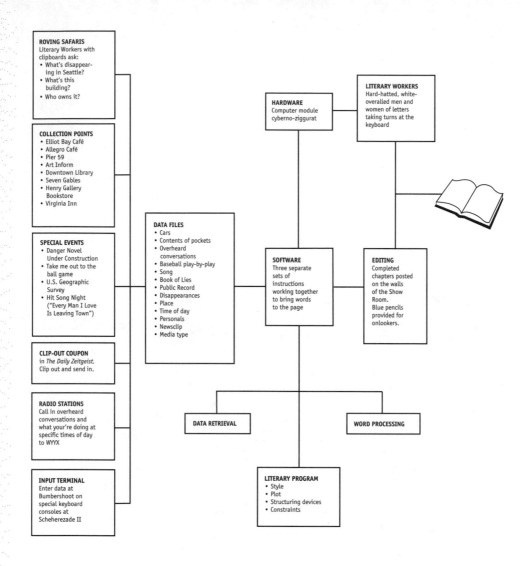

ROVING SAFARIS
Literary Workers with clipboards ask:
- What's disappearing in Seattle?
- What's this building?
- Who owns it?

COLLECTION POINTS
- Elliot Bay Café
- Allegro Café
- Pier 59
- Art Inform
- Downtown Library
- Seven Gables
- Henry Gallery Bookstore
- Virginia Inn

SPECIAL EVENTS
- Danger Novel Under Construction
- Take me out to the ball game
- U.S. Geographic Survey
- Hit Song Night ("Every Man I Love Is Leaving Town")

CLIP-OUT COUPON
in *The Daily Zeitgeist.* Clip out and send in.

RADIO STATIONS
Call in overheard conversations and what your're doing at specific times of day to WYYX

INPUT TERMINAL
Enter data at Bumbershoot on special keyboard consoles at Scheherezade II

DATA FILES
- Cars
- Contents of pockets
- Overheard conversations
- Baseball play-by-play
- Song
- Book of Lies
- Public Record
- Disappearances
- Place
- Time of day
- Personals
- Newsclip
- Media type

HARDWARE
Computer module cyberno-ziggurat

LITERARY WORKERS
Hard-hatted, white-overalled men and women of letters taking turns at the keyboard

SOFTWARE
Three separate sets of instructions working together to bring words to the page

EDITING
Completed chapters posted on the walls of the Show Room. Blue pencils provided for onlookers.

DATA RETRIEVAL

WORD PROCESSING

LITERARY PROGRAM
- Style
- Plot
- Structuring devices
- Constraints

The text flow of Invisible Seattle's Novel Project. While text accumulated in late summer of of 1983, the "first of a new generation of literary computers," Scheherezade II took shape in sculptor Clair Colquitt's studio.

Clair Colquitt

Everett Herald

INVISIBLE SEATTLE
Literary Computer Project
Clearance 5 — Access To Things Dormant for Centuries, Unimaginable in Former Times, or Normally Hidden From the Light of Day

Literary Worker No. 62624

Name_____

Favorite Name Speebus

'Ayes' 2   Knows yes

Hare Br.   Brained 100%

Mollusks are of the Jones family

"I Swear to tell the Truth, More than the Truth and Much More than the Truth"

A team of Literary Workers scoured the city in search of words, phrases, characters, and plot twists. "Pardon me. We're building a novel, may we borrow a couple of your words?"

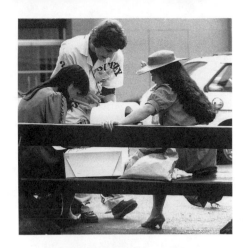

Using questionnaires and fill-in-the-blanks forms, Literary Workers harvested the imagination of the city.

SONG NIGHT - I

<u>Disappear</u>

Disappear!
You make my ~~heart~~ *love* disappear
Your *aura* tells me when you're near
And my ~~blah blah~~ *eyes* starts to _*clear*_ !!

Disappear-- *ulterior* *motive* s are very clear
Your ~~motives~~ *motive* s are very clear
And when you whisper *lets* *hot tub* in my ear
There's just no *love* to _*fear*_ .

(bridge) I used to think ~~that~~ *dope* the city
Was more ~~thrilling~~ *sexy* than *you* ~~person~~ *"U"* is *teasING*
But now that the *real* *"U"*
I think I'll head for the _____

Disappear!
This funny *relationship* is my crazy fear
The whole *mellow* *feeling* just isn't here
Why must we *drown* in the *beer* ??

Come on, whoa, disappear (fade)

Photos: Jane Zalutsky

AUTHOR TO AUTHOR

You Have Read the Prologue, and Examined the Clues — NOW'S YOUR CHANCE!

What is the photograph (fig. 1) a picture of?

The edge of ter...

Where was this picture taken?

Sebestapol, in the Civ...

When was it taken? (What information leads yo...

June 17, 1954 (the...

What would you say is happening in this pictur...

A young woman discovers a question, and...

Respond to any of the speculations raised in th... photo, or add your own speculations. It 4... with the story — a red herr...

What kind of list is this (fig. 2)? The na... members of a secret soc...

How was it made? Carefully, fearful... closed doors, by flashlight.

What could be the connection between these n... of a conspiracy which lacks... Sense of purpose, but does...

Invent a biography for one of the names on the... A born leader, born in Kentucky... nodest means and few pretews.

Whether or not you are a handwriting analyst, d... the signatures. Edith Dan.on is... very depended upon him. A very

Why was this map (fig. 3) devised, and by who... An artist in Bremerton drew it to Lampoon the... the accursed city.

Why did the previous investigator "Proteus" have it? He mistakenly believed it to be a treasure map. Proteus was none too bright.

What happened to Proteus? A double-agent, he was finally liquidated by the forces of darkness.

What was Proteus' mission in Seattle? To throw me off track. The secret I seek is in Portofino, Italy.

Suggest a solution that ties all these clues together with his mission. Idiocy and confusion.

Suggest a way in which his mission is linked to the fate of the city. Seattle is home to the forces of darkness (Martin Selig? Norton (Clore? and so on))

What are some things that are disappearing now in Seattle? What are some ways that things are disappearing? (For example: Immigrants have languages like Norwegian and Laotion that disappear. Money disappears and becomes plastic credit cards. Homes and buildings disappear as their areas become rezoned.) Trees. Skepticism. Provincialism. Good taste. Reserve. Patience. Rational thought. Space needle pencils. Stan Boreson hats. Waffle Stompers. Old pickups.

...d us a newspaper clipping about your fav... ...ley Hoppe)

THE CITY IS TALKING TO YOU -- ALL YOU NEED TO DO IS LISTEN

INVISIBLE SEATTLE

LITERARY COMPUTER PROJECT

1.) Good. You've made it here. A little bit later than we
    expected, but . . . no matter.
2.) Quickly make a cursory survey of the area and establish these
    two items:
    > a) an outdoor place where you can comfortably sit or
    >   stand for several minutes and write.
    > b) determine if there is a restaurant, bar, shop,
    >   deli, etc. reasonably near where you could write
    >   down an interior scene later.
3.) Check your fly to make sure it is in its full, upright position.
    Adjust your badge.
4.) Go to your "Exterior Writing Spot"; get out your "writing mater-
    ials."
5.) Face due North.
6.) Begin to rotate slowly in a counter-clockwise direction,
    writing down everything you see, until you have completed a
    full 360° rotation.
7.) Well . . . not everything . . . enough of the kind of detail
    that would concretely establish the place as a stage
    of action -- and details that would differentiate this neigh-
    borhood from any other.
8.) Describe People and cars that pass by -- what they look like
    ---specifically --- and what they do.
9.) Capture all the words you can see -- all of them -- signs,
    graffiti, bumper stickers, scraps of trash, etc.
10.) Remember you are trying to capture the essence of this
     place for use in an investigation. Note down anything that
     seems suspicious ... or out of place ... or deceptively
     ordinary.
11.) If you are questioned as to your actions, you may reply in a
     polite fashion with a brief description of The Novel. You are
     required, however, to eat these instructions.
12.) Capture the things that are not normally included in books;
     the things that every resident has long ago stopped seeing;
     the things that only a person like yourself, (who has never
     been out of 17th Century Burma before in their life) can
     see -- the invisible obvious.
13.) Write as much as you can -- but remember more -- you may
     be called on to help when as and if your location comes up in
     The Novel.
14.) Now, if there is a suitable location for an interior within
     view proceed there as soon as you are finished with your 360° .
     exterior.
15.) If there is no suitable interior in sight, locomote yourself in
     a likely direction. When you wish to turn, turn in this pattern:
     LEFT LEFT RIGHT LEFT; LEFT LEFT RIGHT LEFT, until you find a
     suitable interior.
16.) Once in the interior - perform another 360° scan with writing.
     Notice particularly visible words, (menus, etc.) and conversations.
17.) You're done -- observation complete. Did anyone bring any lemonade
     ...soda or anything ... I'm thirsty as all heck.

*Literary Workers dispersed around the city, stockpiling place descriptions that would be
ready to go once the four-day, public, novel-drafting marathon began.*

Jane Zalutsky

Once Seattle Mayor Charles Royer had thrown out the opening word, the doors opened on the site of Invisible Seattle's Novel Project. There being no great novel of Seattle, the invisibles proposed that the city write one itself—the Novel of Seattle, by Seattle. For four days, thousands of authors swarmed around the "cyberno-ziggurat" Sheherezade II, reading, writing, and editing.

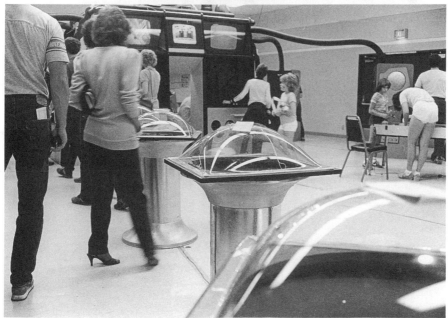

Photos: Paul Dorpat

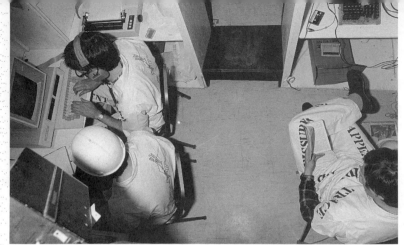

Jake Seniuk

Around Scheherezade II and inside the cabin, the novel takes shape.

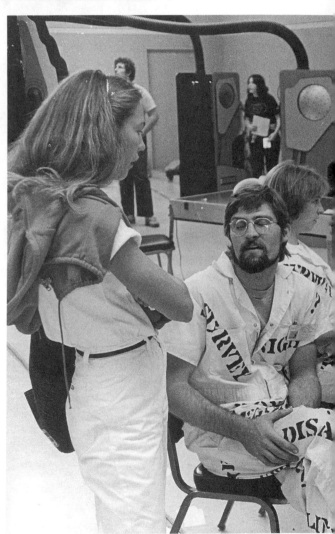

Visitor Ken Kesey adds words to the mix.

Rob Wittig

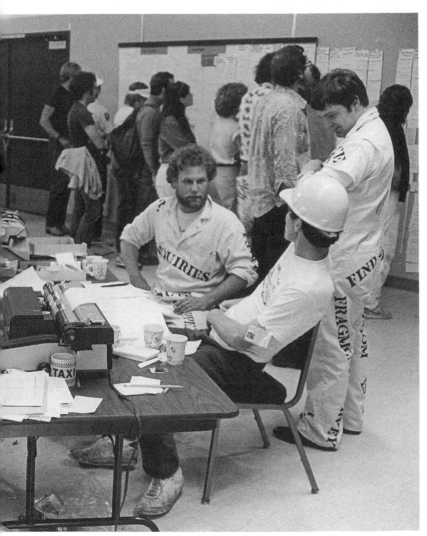

Paul Dorpat

He sells ads for
Art Forum.
He goes to the best parties.
I mean the best parties.

97

"His brain, like a vegetable."

one old jewish woman to
her friend on the bus

97

- "Give me a 4-letter word
  for "soaking flax""

- "Wick"

- "Why?"

97

"...and so this turtle, Eddie
I think, takes off his
underwear and starts
swinging it around his head..."

97

Two older ladies talking
to each other — one saying
to the other, "They can't scare
me, detox doesn't ~~ever~~ pick up
anyone on this side of Denny Way"

*A fragment of the maginificent data base that has provided material for several
incarnations of the Novel of Seattle, by Seattle.*

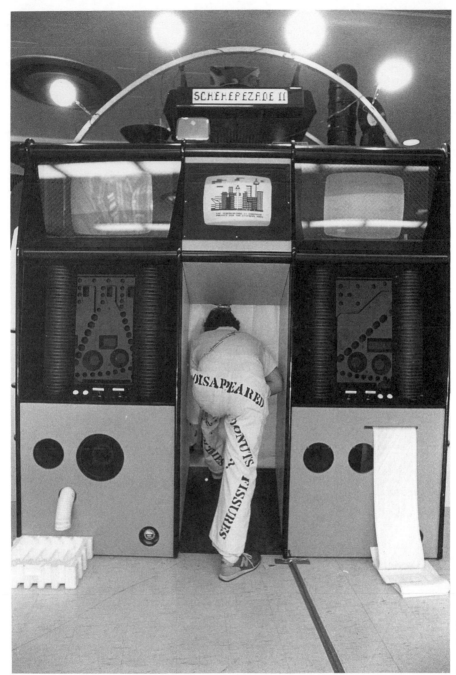

chapter 4

Learning to Write Algorithmically: The Novel Project

"You can't write a novel with a god damned computer!" A waving finger is directed at the Invisible Seattle Literary Worker.

It is August of 1983. A dozen hard-hatted, white-overalled Literary Workers are scampering around a busy downtown intersection gathering data from passersby. "Hi! Were building a novel, may we borrow a few of your words?"

Literary Workers give the intrigued who stop a quick explanation of the project. Contributions of many kinds are to be jotted into notebooks and questionnaires or captured in tape recorders. The public's donations then will be compiled into a novel during the four days of the Bumbershoot Arts Festival on a giant "literary computer" named Scheherezade II.

The initial shyness of the contributors rapidly dissolves. There are smiles, giggles, blurted suggestions. Some finish their novelizing and hurry away, only to rush back with a final phrase.

The harangue continues from the edge of the crowd. "This is bullshit! It'll never work!" Another, more experienced Literary Worker reaches the doubter, pulls him aside and asks "Sir, are you by any chance a writer?" He was, as it often turned out. And even though every effort was made to include his contributions—especially his objections—he stormed off.

This writer's reactions were so vehement because he felt a certain set of structures—a definition of the author, of the work of literature, of the reader—were being threatened by the computer. And they were. Or at least these structures were being interrogated by a team of invisible Literary Workers who were systematically and playfully testing an algorithmic model of literary creation.

Let's return and examine the sources of the algorithmic model that resulted in *Invisible Seattle: The Novel of Seattle, by Seattle* (Invisible Seattle 1987). This algorithmic model was a hybrid of the theatrical past of Invisible Seattle projects, the elegant proofs of the French literary circle Oulipo, and the technology of computers used both as a tool and an analogy.

At its root, the project was a search for pleasure, animated by this question: Where does good writing come from? How does a blank tablet, a blank screen, happen to bear a set of inscriptions that is memorable, moving, something that one bursts to share with friends? The list of models for this process is long. Various deities are said to whisper dictations into the ear of a receptive scribe. Creators of universes are said to place small flickers of their own generative flame in the breasts of those mortals chosen to be geniuses. Individual geniuses, in turn, account for good text.

But the invisibles had been working for several years in an atmosphere of collaboration. The best idea available to improve the work at hand was welcomed, from whatever the source. The model of individual genius seemed less and less viable. How were they to explore this question?

"Don't come to us with any modest proposals," the *Daily Zeitgeist* of 1981 (Invisible Seattle) had called, "with anything that needs funding to 'get off the ground'; we accept only projects that are doomed, absurd, ambitious, sustainable only by faith and energy—in a word, unrealistic."

Operating under the banners of "The Invisible Seattle Literary Computer Project" and "The Novel of Seattle by Seattle," the Novel Project involved some thirty Literary Workers who, for a summer, combed the city in search of novelistic fodder. Stories hit the national press services, camera crews traipsed along on data-gathering expeditions. The culminating event at Bumbershoot was kicked off by Seattle Mayor Charles Royer who donned the white Literary Worker hard-hat, stood at a computer terminal, and threw out the ceremonial first word. By the end of the four days, some 20,000 festival-goers had jammed the room to read, edit, and contribute to the work in progress.

The grand scheme of the Novel Project grew around Christina Wohlstetter's vision of a Bumbershoot event that would be a book signing with a difference. At this book signing everyone who attended would have the right to sign. She imagined a book for which the city telephone book would be the byline.

This sparked a vision of a room bustling with intense "word processing" activity, along the lines of an installation several invisibles had seen at Paris's Centre Georges Pompidou. It was called *The Stock Exchange of the Imaginary* and was clearly inspired by the short-lived Surrealist Research Bureau of the 1920s. Into this exchange poured texts from all points of Paris, reporting daydreams, night dreams, plans, desires, and fantasies.

To accept the challenge of producing the "book that all could sign" meant accepting a horde of interlocking logistical problems.

First, there was the issue of collecting texts. Past brainstorming experience and the civic questionnaires of '82 had shown that satisfying participation relied on a balance between creative focus and creative freedom. Nothing produced more stultifying results than the sloppy invitation to "be creative" and "write whatever you want." So there must be ways of focusing and engaging productive participation.

Next, there was the management issue of dealing with the texts once they came in. Surely there was a better way than a kind of industrial-scale medieval scriptorium with mountains of paper and grueling hand-copying.

Finally, there was a hell of a lot of thinking to do. What form should the book take? Is it possible to build in advance literary structure that does not dictate, but coordinates multiple creativity—an "algorithm" in that word's general sense of "a step-by-step procedure for solving a problem or accomplishing some end?" Many participants in the Novel Project speak fondly of this conceptual aspect of that busy time. "We were constantly placing ourselves in compromising situations," says one Literary Worker.

We spent the summer in a volatile state where we would zero in on certain sacred things about what the novel is, what authors were supposed to do, and try to do just the opposite. If it was supposed to be done alone, we'd do it together. If it was supposed to be private, we'd do it in public. We'd reverse the authority of writer and reader. We'd go interview people on the street and tell them "you're an author, you're an author," and they'd go "no, no," and we'd go "yes, yes."

And the whole time we were talking theory, but not abstractly, like slouching around the seminar table at school, but with a concrete problem right in front of us, with real choices to be made. We were constantly: "What about the copyright?" "Should the characters be illusionistic or self-referential?" "Are we ripping people off?" "Should it even *be* a novel, is that too old-fashioned?" "Who has the right to edit?" "Should it all be in English?" "Are we living up to our claims?"

We came up with a lot more questions than answers. And I think none of us knows quite what to think about the novel, the book at the end, except that it reads good and weird and we've never seen anything like it. The important thing was to have been over our heads in uncharted waters for so long. (manuscript 1992)

The accumulation of texts, dubbed "data gathering," was to happen in a variety of ways. Invisible Seattle Literary Workers deposited questionnaires in spiral binders at libraries, bars, and coffeehouses. They staged data-gathering expeditions to night clubs (where words to a fill-in-the-blanks song were solicited and sung) and baseball games (where multiple fans recorded play-by-play accounts of selected innings).

The first words and images of the Prologue, designed to bring participants quickly into the spirit of the enterprise, were printed in the *Zeitgeist* and handed out at every opportunity, along with a questionnaire.

Seattle, at first glance, is just another American city. Its buildings sit on land that is bought and sold freely. Its streets conduct people to work in the morning and home again at night, giving them no reason to linger. But there is a second city, an "Invisible Seattle," forever taking shape in the fissures and margins of the "visible" city of skyscrapers, donuts, and boredom. Somewhere in this Invisible Seattle lies the answer to the riddle you have been sent to resolve.

Exactly one week ago, your predecessor (a meticulous, thoroughly reliable operative) checked into the very same hotel from which you survey the morning skyline of the city. He made certain inquiries. He kept a diary. He was seen on the waterfront, in the marketplace, at the stadium. On the evening of the fourth day he disappeared without a trace. Your job is to find him—that much is clear—but how? All you have to go on are the objects found in his room. This room. These objects.

A photograph.

A diary.

A list with fourteen names.

A fragment of a map.

A book entitled, without irony, *The Book of Lies*.

The accompanying form asked a series of inciting practical questions about the clues intended to provide a pool of specific characters, motivations, and plots. The most leading question was the following.

> **What are some things that are disappearing now in Seattle? What are some ways that things are disappearing? (For example: Immigrants have languages like Norwegian and Laotian that disappear. Money disappears and becomes plastic credit cards. Homes and buildings disappear as their areas become rezoned.) (Invisible Seattle 1983a)**

The theme of disappearance brought together a number of threads that had occupied the invisibles' thinking over the winter and had resulted in the Prologue. The classic hardboiled detective narrative and the cities it had evoked: New York, San Francisco, L.A.; Alain Robbe-Grillet's experimental novel *Les Gommes* and its literally self-effacing Brussels; the "widening stain" plot pattern where a routine P.I. job leads to increasingly grave revelations until the political and economic underpinnings of the city itself are revealed to be corrupt.

The Book of Lies and the *Diary of Proteus* were to be books within the book for which the episodic, listed texts sure to result from data gathering were formally plausible. A grab-bag of detail was elicited above the mailing address at the end of the questionnaire:

> **Here are some other things you can send in: fragments of overheard conversation, used lottery tickets, cash machine receipts (you can cross out your account number), itemized grocery receipts, a one-line description of your car, or of yourself, or of a loved one.**
>
> **It's your city**
>
> **It's your book (Invisible Seattle 1983a)**

One strand of questioning was designed to map the web of simultaneous events within which individual characters navigate.

"What were you doing yesterday at: 4:10 A.M.; 5 :27 A.M.; 7:41 A.M. . . ." one notebook asked for the fifteen times of day chosen for the novel's fifteen chapters.

But how to accommodate all the outpourings of text it was hoped would come in? How to manage the data?

Sculptor Clair Colquitt appeared at an Invisible Seattle open meeting at the big table at Elliott Bay Café with a paper grocery bag under his arm. From it he pulled what looked like a flattened adding machine with a miniature typewriter keyboard. The cheap plastic case of the machine was pierced with homemade wiring. A one-line liquid crystal display began asking questions. "If you were a conquering general, which downtown building would be your headquarters?" "Where is the best place to hide in public?" "Where does a guy go to get killed around here?" One after another the invisibles pecked in answers, which were immediately printed on a silvery roll of adding machine paper coiling from the back of the machine.

The fact that none of the invisibles had recognized the object in the paper bag as a computer reveals not only their beginner status in the realm of hardware but also the explosively changing state of the technology in 1983, the dawning days of the personal computer. The invisibles had realized early on that computing in some form would be valuable, if not necessary, to the project they had devised. They had begun calling text "data" and spoke of gathering contributions in "data files." The time had come to find out what this really entailed.

The process of educating themselves in computer technology was matched step-by-step by a process of rethinking writing, of overturning one after another the fears many writers had associated with The Machine.

The crash course began with an examination of what the group already knew. It knew phototypesetting.

During the late 1970s a transition was under way from hot lead type to a computer that used light and lenses to expose letter forms onto photographic paper. By 1980, companies such as Compugraphic and AM were making machines the size of a solid bureaucratic desk affordable to small print shops and community newspapers. Jobs in these kinds of industry are exactly the kinds of places young people with degrees in literature landed when they got out of school. The invisibles were no exception.

For a couple of years the Thursday night Invisible Seattle salons had become the site of the creation of a parody romance novel, *Spawning Grounds: or A Romance of a*

Woman Alone in the Frozen North (Fairpipe 1981–1983), under the artistic direction of Janet Skeels. The monthly episodes appeared under the *nom de plume* Jessica Fairpipe in the redoubtable local tabloid, *Voice of the Singles Life*, where an invisible was employed as typesetter. Texts on sheets of yellow legal paper in as many as ten different hands were scooped up from the crowded living room, keyed into the machine, and smoothed into typographic uniformity.

The experience of compiling and editing on-screen was carefully reported to the group. Ah, the pleasures of scrolling, switching paragraphs, trying adjectives on for size, jumping from end to beginning!

Imagine—a text is suspended in a place apart from paper, in a liquid state, where copies, deletions, and alternate orderings are possible with a keystroke. The screen as writing space was forgiving, flexible, intimate. A magnificent setting for sketching, doodling, testing phrases and ideas. Ah, the delicious guilt of wasting the time of an expensive machine!

The invisibles had been smitten by the pleasures of word processing—this would change forever what it felt like to write—and then treated to the astonishment of going straight from the glowing screen to galleys of rich, official type!

The group found a company willing to sponsor them in the form of two loaned desktop word processing machines that provided the heart of the literary computer, Scheherezade II. More important, they had already bypassed the single biggest humanistic objection to the use of the computer in literature—a fundamental fear of the machine.

In contrast to the menace of centralized computing as portrayed by Hollywood in the '60s and '70s (inheritor of the mantle of centralized heavy industry from films such as *Metropolis* and *Modern Times*), the invisibles had already been exposed to distributed, "personal" computing. They had experienced the computer as tool—a rather bumbling and unthreatening tool in those days—instead of computer as secret police or computer as slavemaster. Surely there could be no harm to the creative process from using a machine like the one that cranked out *Spawning Grounds* every month. In fact, it had clearly abetted this pleasurable collaboration.

But what of the notion of writing as a natural process, one tainted by the artificiality of the machine? Discussions surrounding the Robbins trial had made much of the word "natural,"—the good, natural country vs. the bad, artificial city—finding that it was the most commonly used word in the advertising of that year. Now it appeared that "natural" was the key word in a string of ancient objections that had sought to discredit technologies of writing through movable type back to the days of the ancient Greeks. To see these arguments repeated time and again, at the advent of each new technology, was to defuse them. As George Landow comments in his book *Hypertext: The Convergence of Contemporary Critical Theory and Technology* (1992), "All the self-proclaimed Luddites in academe turn out to oppose only the newest machines, not machines in general and certainly not machines that obviate human drudgery" (168).

Computers destroy nothing, the invisibles decided, but the veil the Romantics had drawn over writing to dramatize its processes.

The material of the novel-to-be began to be considered in a deromanticized, demystified, material way—words, plot ideas, data to be elicited, stored, and later recombined. The invisibles had already begun parlor writing experiments in which they carried the habits of *Spawning Grounds* even further. They offered up their own writing to be hacked, altered, and even interleaved on the sentence level with selections from a delicious volume from 1917, Grenville Kleiser's *Fifteen Thousand Useful Phrases*.

But most of all they were beginning to lay a structure, an organized blueprint for a good novel. What was at stake was not simply a one-time event, an exercise in local boosterism, but a procedure that could be repeated in other times by other cities. What was at stake was potential literature.

So when the group was introduced to the work of the Oulipo, the timing couldn't have been better.

The organization Oulipo was founded in France in 1960 by the writer and Transcendent Satrap of the Collège de Pataphysique Raymond Queneau and Mathematician François Le Lionnais. The best definition of the group's name is given by American Oulipean Harry Mathews.

Oulipo stands for Ouvroir de littérature potentielle: both "'workshop' and 'sewing circle' of potential literature"—"sewing circle" in its old meaning of a place where well-to-do ladies made clothes for the poor. This word was chosen to

indicate, with self-depreciating irony, the communal, beneficial nature of the Oulipo's work. "Potential" was preferred to "experimental," because what matters to the Oulipo is the literature it makes possible rather than what it actually realizes. (Mathews 1991, 173)

Prime mover Queneau succinctly defined potential literature as "the search for new forms and structures which may be used by writers in any way they see fit" (Queneau cited in Motte 1986, xi). For over thirty years these new forms have been shared over monthly feasts among a group whose members have included Mathews, Georges Perec, Jacques Roubaud, Italo Calvino, and Marcel Duchamp. The initial near-secrecy of the group's production has ceded over the years to increasing, but always modest and slyly mischievous, publication and outreach. Warren Motte's 1986 anthology of translations *Oulipo: A Primer of Potential Literature*, is an excellent handbook of basic Oulipean ideas and forms.

The first and perennially cited example of potential literature is Queneau's *Cent Mille Milliards de poèmes* (*One Hundred Thousand Billion Poems*) (1961). Ten sonnets are printed in a book with cut paper that allows each line of each sonnet to turn separately. The number of possible sonnets—all of which rhyme properly, all of which flow grammatically from line to line—is given in the title.

Nearly every introduction to the Oulipo begins by explaining the Oulipean procedure called N + 7 (in French, S + 7), and for good reason. It is a simple rule that produces quick and gratifying results. Italianism is a simple rumen that produces quick and gratifying resurrectionists.

N + 7 means simply that every noun in a given text is to be replaced by the seventh noun following it in a given dictionary. (Mathews 1991, 177)

N + 7 also exemplifies the Oulipo's attitude toward language. Mathews again provides the most elegant formula in the first lines of his procedure, *Mathews's Algorithm*.

From the reader's point of view, the existence in literature of potentiality in its Oulipean sense has the charm of introducing duplicity into all written texts, whether Oulipean or not. It isn't merely a sonnet in Queneau's *One Hundred Thousand Billion Poems* on which doubt is cast by the horde of alternatives waiting to take its place: the most practical work of prose, no matter how sturdy it may seem in its apparent uniqueness, will prove just as fragile as soon as one thinks of subjecting it to the procedures of N + 7 or Semo-Definitional

Literature. Beyond the words being read, others lie in wait to subvert and perhaps surpass them. Nothing any longer can be taken for granted; every word has become a banana peel. The fine surface unity that a piece of writing proposes is belied and beleaguered; behind it, in the realm of potentiality, a dialectic has emerged. (Mathews 1991, 187)

When Oulipean Georges Perec's 1969 novel *La Disparition* (*The Disappearance*) was published, it was hailed for the resolute modernity of its haunting style. What at least one critic failed to notice was that its 300 pages were written entirely without use of the letter "E" (a feat even more daunting in French than it is in English). This procedure, the refusal of a letter, is called the "lipogram." In his essay, "The History of the Lipogram," Perec is at pains to point out that the history of the constraint of removing a letter dates back as far as the sixth century B.C. He goes on to decry the critical neglect of these adventurous writers of the past.

"Exclusively preoccupied with its great capitals (Work, Style, Inspiration, World-Vision, Fundamental Options, Genius, Creation, etc.), literary history seems deliberately to ignore writing as practice, as work, as play. Systematic artifices, formal mannerisms (that which, in the final analysis, constitutes Rabelais, Sterne, Roussel . . .) are relegated to the registers of asylums for literary madmen." (Perec in Motte 1986, 5)

The Oulipeans had discovered that systems of formal constraint laid out in advance of a work's composition could have a liberating, rather than limiting, effect. Founder Queneau placed primary importance on literature's voluntary nature, "inspiration which consists in blind obedience to every impulse is in reality a sort of slavery." (Queneau in Benabou, Motte 1986, 41)

Masterful novels such as Perec's *Life A User's Manual* (1987), and Calvino's *If on a Winter's Night a Traveler* (1981) are examples of constellations of Oulipean constraints deployed within the covers of a bound book.

Their willingness to take a demystified, mechanistic view of the literary process and their alliance with mathematics give the Oulipeans a uniquely dispassionate perspective on the involvement of computers in literature.

One Hundred Thousand Billion Poems is exemplary of a work that may benefit from but does not depend on computers. The concept begs to be programmed, as it finally was by Paul Braffort in the 1980s. The important point is that as a text, the ten sonnets along with their instructions conjure up a Borgesian apparition. Even if you had the million-plus centuries Queneau estimated it would take to read all the versions, it wouldn't matter whether you read it on a computer or not. For potential literature the computer is beside the point.

But what of the possibility of computer-generated texts, of a computer author?

Having laid down these procedures and entrusted a computer with the task of carrying out these operations, will we have a machine capable of replacing the poet and the author?

Oulipean Italo Calvino, as usual, goes to the heart of the problem.

The interesting thing is not so much the question of whether this problem is soluble in practice—because in any case it would not be worth the trouble of constructing such a complicated machine—as the theoretical possibility of it, which would give rise to a series of unusual conjectures. . . . I am thinking of a writing machine that would bring to the page all those things that we are accustomed to consider as the most jealously guarded attributes of our psychological life, of our daily experience, our unpredictable changes of mood and inner elations, despairs and moments of illumination. What are these if not so many linguistic "fields," for which we might well succeed in establishing the vocabulary, grammar, syntax, and properties of permutation? (Calvino 1986, 12)

The invisibles' response to this possibility was to act as though a convincing computer author already existed. But as none was at hand, they continued the conceptual planning of the Novel Project now armed with Oulipean methods.

As the Bumbershoot Arts Festival drew nearer, it became clear that the four-day "novel composition" event would be a hybrid of algorithmic thinking and 18th-century technologies. The invisibles had had neither time nor budget enough to attempt the programming that would result in a fully automated Scheherezade II. Despite the able efforts of the technical advisors, there was going to be plenty of "manually plotted data storage" (handwriting) and "Adidas networking" (walking floppy disks from one machine to another).

The novel was to have fifteen chapters. "You," the second-person protagonist, was to return to home base, the derelict William Penn hotel, in chapters one, five, ten, and fifteen. Settings for the remaining eleven chapters need to be described by Bumbershoot's opening day.

Invisible Seattle gathered at noon in the dark College Inn Pub where a map of the city had been placed over the dartboard. Darts flew, locations were called out, and teams of Literary Workers were dispatched around the city, bearing sealed envelopes. Upon breaking the seals, they discovered a set of step-by-step instructions for producing a verbal record of the place.

Text of all kinds was accumulating in binders, bags, cardboard boxes. Piece by piece the great cowling of the central module of Scheherezade II was brought to the Bumbershoot grounds. The four data-gathering pods (converted video arcade games), were placed around the central module, ready to ask their questions and collect their answers. The clues (the list, photo, map, etc., of the Prologue) were placed under their protective display bubbles.

The *Rules of the Game* (Wittig 1983) spelled out the mechanics of the event that the group had developed, a kind of relay race rotating invisible compilers, called "Guest Writers," into chairs at the keyboards and funnelling the growing flow of contributions.

The *Guest Writers' Guidelines*, a distillation of the summer's algorithmic preparations, were posted above the word processor keyboards in Scheherazade II's main cabin.

4. The second person singular should be used to create a distance, to avoid the easy identifications of "first-person hardboiled." The "You" is a character, a set of instructions to the reader, a series of possibilities.

5. Terry Lawson, third name on the list, has become the love interest, will meet "You" casually, will gradually become deeply involved, will force an emotional climax—and will never identify himself, sorry, herself, sorry . . . will never be identified definitively as a man or woman despite the graphic detail about Terry's arms, lips, hair, etc. Strategies to conceal the disappearance of the third person pronoun will become ever more playful and baroque, perhaps even involving erasures or comments like: "h . . . (two illegible letters here) voice was low and thrilling." (Wohlstetter 1983)

The physical design of Scheherezade II emphasized the coexistence of the book world with the electronic world—monitors, video screens on the sides, bookshelves on the ends, and a popcorn popper on top. The cabin was large enough to contain three or four Literary Workers at a time, who were visible to the public through the small hatches. What the architecture presented to the visitors was a 3-D diagram of an algorithmic way of thinking.

Once the doors were opened and the authors flooded in, the Novel Project became an exhilarating madhouse. Raw data and drafts soon covered the walls, where visitors read, laughed, and exercised their blue pencils. Any sense of schedule was blown in the first hours. Piles of paper data were shoveled into the Scheherezade's cabin like coal into a steam engine. Guest writers leaned out of the hatches in search of a detail, flagging down the first passing author. Printed chapters snaked through the slot and out onto the floor; popcorn tumbled down the chute and into bags. By the end of four days (in fact, early on the morning of the fifth) the city had a draft of its novel.

What reviewers of *Invisible Seattle: The Novel of Seattle, by Seattle* got, (reviewers of Version 7.1 that is, published by Function Industries Press in 1987, the most widely distributed version) was not what they expected. It struck both too high and too low. Instead of fiction in the *New Yorker* or "little literary review" mold, the result was a flagrant, multi-genre collision involving the nouveau roman, a Dos Passos/Joycean catalog of particulars, the pulp detective/thriller genre, careful historiography, and a full load of what one kind commentator termed "*je ne sais* the fuck *quoi*."

Those who participated in this spectacle from its beginnings were marked forever by it. A new image of the process of writing had replaced the Romantic one in their minds—an image of a room full of people creating within a frame of rules, reaching into big cardboard boxes for handfuls of text as needed, giving away ideas, reading fragments aloud, delighting in the prose of others, trying chunks of text in variant orders, editing in teams, writing in public for all to see.

For invisibles thus marked, the step onto IN.S.OMNIA a few months later was a small one. In September of 1984 an IN.S.OMNIA user looked back on the lessons of the Novel Project.

If I had a nickel for all the sleepless nights I've spent agonizing over putting the novel Invisible Seattle into its final form. . . . But I have seen the error of my ways.

There cannot be one, authorized version of the novel, just as no one, neat glossy version of the city is the city.

The in.s.omniac then describes the results of the year's collaborative editing process: from lists of data, to straightforward narrative, to a nonsequential narrative of alternative possibilities, back to a form based on lists!

We had to go all the way through the "noveling" process to realize that there was a different literary form being revealed for future use. Perhaps a do-it-yourself story kit (more like the facsimile dossier detective novels with the actual cigarette butts and locks of hair in plastic bags that we looked at in the early meetings). Perhaps a bunch of materials you cruise around in, as though in a city on a three-day visit, the monuments staying neatly in their places (lists), and you creating the narrative out of the attractive person you meet in the bookstore, the fight at the library, the open manhole.

What we wound up with was not a novel, or better to say more than a novel; we wound up with a data base of material from which many different, polished, presentable subworks can be made. . . . We knew we wanted to "mock the notion of a single author." We didn't know that, in addition, we were mocking the notion of "completion by authorial fiat," of a work crystallized at the point of perfection. We have on our hands a loose-leaf novel, a *Leaves of Grass* novel, a data base novel! Long live "You!" Long live "Terry!" (Invisible Seattle 1987, 246)

The threat that moved the writer on the street to yell at the Literary Workers was a perception of these remappings. And we sympathize; we too have fond memories of the old neighborhood: the attractive genius, the typeset masterpiece, the obedient reader.

But it was a mistake to make computer technology the villain. For the invisibles, the computer was a happy solution to problems they had begun to pose long before.

The great change still under way is in modes of thinking, not merely about computers, but about the entire functioning of culture. There is a reimagining under way of the natural and the artificial, a redefinition of the qualifications of creators of culture, a new understanding of how culture is produced and enjoyed. There is an awareness that, beneath the mystical descriptions of the writing process, there has always been algorithmic planning involved. Evidence of such thinking surrounds us, in all media. Far from being a cultural avant-garde, the literary world is, at this point, among the last to absorb this transformation.

exempli gratia v

The R'evolution Room

. . . joining the game in progress . . .

▌8 5 j u l 1 7   f r o m   E u g e n e   C o r r e c t
I hope the last few contributors to this room die soon. Function, you
have the IQ of a monotreme. The captain you're talking about was
named NEMO ("omen" spelled backwards, get it?), whom Walt Disney
brought to fame after discovering him in a science ed film, "Nemo the
Magnificent."▌

▌8 5 j u l 1 7   f r o m   E r i c   S c h m i d t
Obviously your wit is only exceeded by your scientific knowledge. That
star of stage and school room was "HEMO the magnificent" whose next
film was done with a lye-based material that is used to clear clogged
plumbing (or the carotid arteries of some contributors).▌

▌8 5 j u l 1 7   f r o m   M e h i t a b e l
What a bunch of Nemo-toads and Neo-nerds, not to mention pomo-
phobes and, and, dUMMIES. Maroons abound in this world. Luckily for
you there are real smart people like I to straighten you out. DRANO is
the word for which you unsuccessfully plumbed your offline storage, as
in those beautiful blond horses like Trigger.▌

▌8 5 j u l 1 8   f r o m   A n i   V e r n a z z a
No, no, no, Mehit, the burden of intelligence hasn't weighed heavily
upon you for some time. The word that you want is PALOMINO, the
fuzzy black and white bears whose sexual misadventures delight so
many visitors to the National Zoo.▌

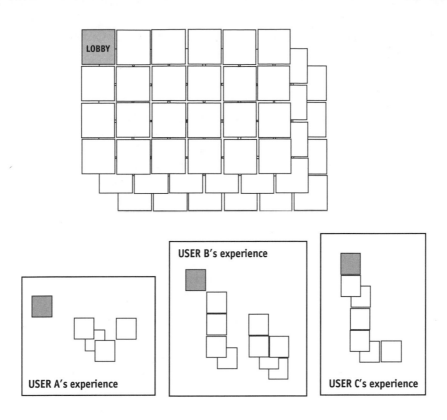

Use of IN.S.OMNIA. Each user selects, reads, and contributes to a unique bulletin board with each call.

▌85jul18 from Ken Coller
But they are more raccoons than bears, O person of the anagrammatic name. You refer to PANDAs, which are not even remotely bears, but would no doubt know that these stringily extruded filaments of starch find themselves in the company of sauces favored by Il Duce and Karol W. (the pope) Vicar.▌

▌85jul18 from Clair
H-A . . . surely O mister Ken Collar person the tiny particle of brain that has become cruelly lodged in the vacuum of the enormous cavity situated beneath your poorly maintained Kanekolon duster has caused your troubled countenance to project the falsehood of a term that had the correct description been made would reveal that PASTA is the true key to your ill tested definition, and on deeper involvement with the very meaning of the offending noun we can see that we can indeed find using said word that it is fully adequate for purposes of explaining the lineage of a certain male that has had the misfortune of being born out of wedlock. Please DO take care with the accuracy by which you

husband such faulty logic, and deal with as much precision as has been my care to take.▌

▌8 5 j u l 1 9   f r o m   M i k e   R o b i n s o n
Clair, you imbecilic maroon. Your obscure and falsely authenticated lineage is embarrassing you and your readers! If your parents had not been related to each other, your brain would have developed enough to realize that the word you are trying to define is BASTARD. However, since your childhood neighborhood rarely hosted any motorized vehicles that were not on blocks next to one's front porch, we will forgive the fact that you are unaware that this word describes a commodity relished by owners of fine touring cars.▌

▌8 5 j u l 1 9   f r o m   C l a r k   H u m p h r e y
Mike, Mike, when it comes to brains the slogan "Ask the Man Who Owns One" obviously applies not to you. For otherwise, you would have understood that a PACKARD is a professional athlete from the verdant state of Wisconsin.▌

▌8 5 j u l 1 9   f r o m   S y s t e m   O p e r a t o r
My sources tell me that Clark is to be forgiven his ignorance. It seems he gets most of his advice from extra-terrestrials. PACKERS, as we all know, are those computer nerdies who stay up late at night cutting lines of code for cheap thrills. (IN.S.OMNIA)▌

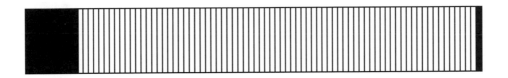

Use of a book as it is commonly conceived. The reader dutifully trudges the linear track prescribed by the author.

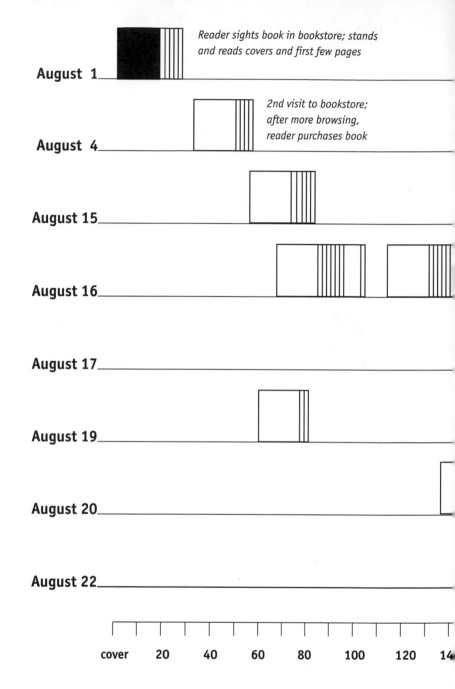

Reader sights book in bookstore; stands and reads covers and first few pages

2nd visit to bookstore; after more browsing, reader purchases book

August 1

August 4

August 15

August 16

August 17

August 19

August 20

August 22

cover 20 40 60 80 100 120 14

Use of a book in reality. Case study: a book recommended by an acquaintance.

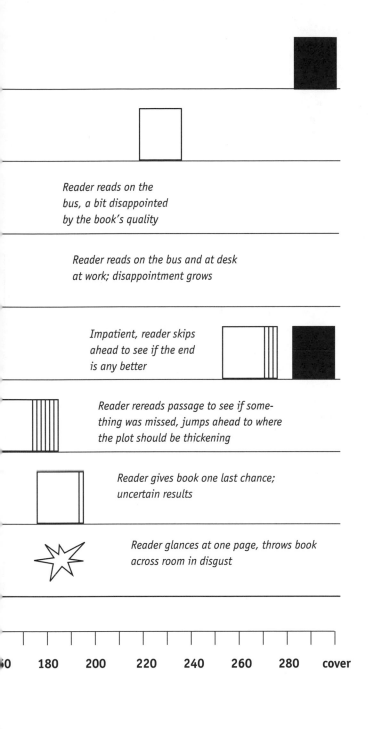

Reader reads on the
bus, a bit disappointed
by the book's quality

Reader reads on the bus and at desk
at work; disappointment grows

Impatient, reader skips
ahead to see if the end
is any better

Reader rereads passage to see if something was missed, jumps ahead to where
the plot should be thickening

Reader gives book one last chance;
uncertain results

Reader glances at one page, throws book
across room in disgust

| 180 | 200 | 220 | 240 | 260 | 280 | cover |

Notes for a new Medium (or) Is There Life After Literature?

1. Begin with a description of the IN.S.OMNIA BBS (Bulletin Board System). An IBM-PC sitting on Gyda's desk in the Scandinavian quarter of Seattle. The modem that links it to a phone 24 hours a day. How anybody else with a computer and modem can call up IN.S.OMNIA and read or leave texts. No tech talk though. No bilge about "the electronic world of tomorrow" or "revolution in literature" etc.

2. Something about the software. How it structures the BBS into "rooms." How each "room" or topic offers a series of successive dated messages that scroll vertically line by line across your screen. How you can stop the message, jump to the next one, enter a new message, jump to the next "room," scan the messages there.

3. The intangibles. Experience of reading off a screen. Rhythms. Speed of scroll. The effect of the different user "Nyms" (Pseudo, Epo, Hetero) as each writer splits Pessoa-like into multiple personas not attached to a solid, tangible, imaginable author-authority.

4. Some reflections on new modes of dissemination. Compare to MAIL ART. Both it and BBS reunite the activities of Reading/Writing and Production/Consumption generally separated by a host of middlemen—writer's agent, editor, marketer. You address other human beings who WRITE and READ, not some mute segment of amass market designated as "Audience." You are the audience, the auditor, the speaker, the reader, the writer—constantly shifting gears, enjoying all roles.

5. Possibilities beyond mere use as publishing medium. A workshop. An ideal writing laboratory. Site for Oulipean games, collaborative ventures within agreed-upon formal structures,

warming-up exercises before the return to the more tradition-
ally conceived solitary literary pursuit, which continues to
exist side by side, though mysteriously altered. Dissolves the
"university writing class"—spoken critique of your work as
social embarrassment lurks—replacing your needless presence
with the absence of voice that is writing responding to other
writing.

6. A true "Republic of Letters." Anyone can play, skilled or
   unskilled, pro or am. Our habitual users: visual artists, anthro-
   pologists, programmers, etc. as well as literary gents and gen-
   tlewomen. And the unknowns just passing by who leave their
   words behind. A sense that there is always someone else
   about to arrive and astonish us. You.

7. Derridean project. What possible adventures are left for the
   written word? What is writing outside the book ("the end of
   the book and the beginning of writing")? Historical excursus
   to stress how brief a period we've entrusted our words, our
   secrets, to the enclosured page. Other graphic supports: walls,
   rocks, subway cars. And now the flickering green screen. The
   words never solidly inscribed or scratched but luminous,
   unstable, evanescent, cast out upon the black lagoon of the
   screen by a pseudonymous, anonymous, eponymous scriptor.

8. "Literature"—a club wielded to prevent such experiments as
   this (as in "Yes, but it's not L . . . "). "Art"—fetish of the
   closed, polished object designed for eager consumers.
   "Writing"—ah, now we're getting closer to what is after all a
   basic human activity indulged in with greater or lesser degrees
   of intelligence and delight by many good Americans to whom
   IN.S.OMNIA offers a perennial invitation to inscribe a first
   word and follow wherever it will lead. (*Invisible Seattle's
   Omnia* 1985, 1)

Sampling and Linking: IN.S.OMNIA and the Habits of Hypertext

In the months after the culminating event of the Novel Project at Bumbershoot, the IN.S.OMNIA electronic network was put into operation. At the same time—in a rooftop studio shared with painters and sculptors above Seattle's downtown YMCA—the thousands of scraps of the Novel of Seattle in their cardboard boxes were being put through an elaborate, collaborative editing process. This was "editing" much more in the sense of the post-production phase of filmmaking than traditional literary editing. It was collaborative and combinatory.

During this period of going back and forth between the "platforms" of the Novel Project and IN.S.OMNIA, a discovery was made: Shuffling and sharpening physical pieces of text from the novel and shuffling and composing messages in IN.S.OMNIA's data base were the same activity. Part selection, part connection, part composition, this activity consisted of linking disparate scraps of existing material and forming a new constellation. Once it had been discerned, the same activity could be seen operating in large portions of the culture—music, broadcasting, performance, micropublishing.

The long-distance investigations of the first years of IN.S.OMNIA were, in part, playful explorations of the activity of linking.

The paradigmatic "atom" of the cultural landscape of atoms waiting to be formed into molecules is the IN.S.OMNIA system's basic building block, the "message."

(in the "Tristram's Shanty Room")
86may13 from The Wangler
A MEDITATION ON 1968
Patchouli, incense, weekly casualty reports from Vietnam, blacklights, and the
sound of an electric sitar . . . words such as these and approximately 300 more

can fit into the short, 1,968-character memory buffer of an IN.S.OMNIA message. What used to seem like a dratted inconvenience—just as you get rolling the system stops receiving copy and says BUFFER FULL, forcing you to divide long texts into tiny segments—now seems entirely appropriate to Sterne and his Tristram, whose book divides and multiplies constantly into small outgrowths topped by blocky roman numerals. It's interesting to be forced by the 1,968 buffer into short-chapter-sized meditations . . . of course you can string them along in great chains, writing CONT. CONT. CONT. (a word we would blush to pronounce) obsessively at the top of each morsel . . . (IN.S.OMNIA)

The effect of IN.S.OMNIA's draconian maximum message length is to make the bulletin board a field of small texts, all more or less equal in size and graphic presentation, each with its own name/date stamp at the top.

In time, after daily use, "message" length becomes the norm. Long passages seem like independent messages strung together instead of whole texts unnaturally chopped apart. Users create approximations of print-world genres by combining the atoms of messages into the molecules of stories or essays. Synthetic genres coalesce in the electronic laboratory like polyesters.

Having seen text sliced and diced changes for all time an in.s.omniac's vision of the print world. The printed matter surrounding a regular user begins to come apart in a hallucinatory swirl of small messages, each eager to nuzzle up against unexpected new friends. The user recognizes in these messages the *lexia* of Barthes, the *topic* (from the eminently geographic Greek root *topos*) of Jay David Bolter's book *Writing Space: The Computer, Hypertext, and the History of Writing* (1991).

On IN.S.OMNIA all text is managed in terms of messages. This practice of writing as "message linking" has a certain number of seductive properties.

Although the entering of messages is a private matter, the field on which they are arrayed is immediately public. Users are only partially in control of what other messages surround a given entry. This changes a user's sense of ownership. Messages on IN.S.OMNIA have the intriguing quality of being treated as common property, like words themselves, ripe for recombination into new orders, new forms.

In theory (although rarely in IN.S.OMNIA practice) messages can be moved from room to room and put into new sequences. This throws issues of sequencing into a new light, casting doubt on notions of necessary or organic ordering.

Playing in this field of interchangeable messages becomes, above all, an act of combining. When new messages are needed to achieve a particular effect—to finish a particular molecule—users will supply them, in the words of "Big Phone" Bill, "even if we have to write them ourselves."

In.s.omniacs thrash around for analogies in an attempt to describe their behavior. Building with Lego™ blocks says one. Stringing beads says another. Writing telegrams. Playing telephone. They talk of the bulletin board as a giant crossword puzzle, and of leaving messages as filling in squares. A user takes an existing message as a starting point, another as an ending, and sets herself the task (*à la* Raymond Roussel) of writing the story that goes in between. Gone is the sense of literary creation as the plenishment of any empty page. IN.S.OMNIA is quite matter-of-factly what poststructuralist theory contends all writing is: an exchange already in progress.

The bound codex, the book you hold in your hands, has always been its own best diagram. To know the object is to understand the structure. There has rarely been a need for external graphic representation of how a book works, and overviews of a book's contents can be shown in a simple table.

Electronic text, on the other hand, takes place inside microchips that, although they look suggestively like miniature cities, offer little diagrammatic help in understanding their functions. Our culture—mature in the skills of writing, but less conscious of its graphic abilities—is suddenly faced with the necessity of constructing diagrams in order to map the message linking that is now in full swing. Flowcharts, webs, and other adapted forms offer a beginning, but more is needed.

One promising visual and verbal tool for understanding message thinking is found in Italo Calvino's novel *The Castle of Crossed Destinies* (1976).

In Calvino's tale, travelers take shelter for the night at a castle in the heart of the forest. They find to their dismay that the forest has struck them dumb. Gathered around a table, they begin to lay out tarot cards in order to tell the others who they are and what has brought them there. By the end the narrator writes,

The square is now entirely covered with cards and with stories. My story is also contained in it, though I can no longer say which it is, since their simultaneous interweaving has been so close. In fact, the task of deciphering the stories one

by one has made me neglect until now the most salient peculiarity of our way of narrating, which is that each story runs into another story . . . bearing in mind that the same cards, presented in a different order, often change their meaning . . . (Calvino 1976, 41)

Bulletin boards, like all new forms of culture, quickly develop their own aesthetics in day-to-day practice. The aesthetic at work on IN.S.OMNIA is fierce and demanding. It is impatient with banality, effusive in its praise of success, pitiless in its search for certain pleasures. The aesthetics of "message linking" have roots in the world of print literature. But the roles and structure of the print world are of limited help to in.s.omniacs as they try to heighten their pleasure and perfect their skills.

Right under our noses there are other cultural activities that provide better analogies for understanding an electronic bulletin board.

Popular recorded music is, par excellence, a practice of recombined, or linked, fragments. Radio stations and nightclubs are public fields where songs are constantly put into new juxtapositions. To whom music on the radio or on MTV *belongs* is difficult to determine. The act of combining in these public spaces becomes a conscious practice, differentiating radio stations from one another and making night club deejays stars in their own right.

Nobody bats an eye when musicians record "cover" versions of other musicians' songs. Imagine the same in a literary context, Mailer's *Moby Dick* for example, or Ashbery's *Don Juan*. Not that it hasn't happened in literature (Rabelais's *Gargantua* being a cover version of a down-and-dirty little *Gargantua* book he came across), but the idea tends to violate modern norms of originality.

Les Paul's development of multi-track recording brought a concept of "message linking" into the recording studio early on. Beyond simple cover versions, major music acts frequently have their songs remixed into longer, more danceable, versions to be played in clubs. The most prestigious remixers are known by name and have followings of their own. They take astounding liberties with the original versions, reinstating tracks that were recorded but edited out, adding additional instruments, taking inconsequential passages and turning them into insistent riffs.

"Wouldn't you love to see *The Waste Land* remixed?" asks in.s.omniac Strange Justice.

Somebody needs to scoop up the pieces that Ezra Pound left on the cutting room floor, get behind a big electronic console and hack that mother to bits! April is the cruelest month Ape-Ape-Ape-Ape-April! Phlebas the Phoenician Phlebas, Phlebas, Phlebas the Phoenician Fun-Fun-Fun-Phoenician! (IN.S.OMNIA 1991)

With the hip-hop style that began to develop in the late 1970s, existing songs were chopped into messages, or "breaks." Two copies of a favorite record were cued up to the same break on two nightclub turntables. The deejay would wind the records back by hand, alternating the fragment until it became a solid beat.

The advent of digital sampling (computer storage and playback of fragments of sound) has turned this simple vinyl practice into an explosion of creative possibilities, with hundreds of "sampled" messages available at the touch of a finger. The best current hip-hop pieces are carefully curated retrospectives, combining fragments that evoke whole songs, whole eras, and bristle with wit and irony.

How different breaks and samples are from citations in a book! Citations are imported for many reasons, but too rarely out of the kind of pure pleasure and love that samples represent. Even when citations are loved, they are handled like dangerous isotopes, with lead kid gloves, carefully referenced, scrupulously kept intact. Musical samples are treated casually, familiarly. No references are given—you either recognize them or you don't. By literary standards, samples are treated cavalierly, chopped and mutilated and wrenched from context *as though their reusers had a right to them*.

It is exactly this sense of having a right to recombine existing messages—and by extension all existing text, all existing culture—that users of IN.S.OMNIA come to feel.

The idea of an active user—linking with abandon—is nowhere so apparent as when a home TV viewer grabs the remote control.

Although advertisers and executives know better than anyone the fickleness of the viewer, television programming still clings to the ideal of the movie-theater experience, imagining that viewers watch a single work from beginning to end. Programs are conceived, discussed, and reviewed according to this principle.

In fact, the living room couch has arguably become the throne of Surrealism Triumphant. Armed with a remote control, stocked with a cableful of channels, the home viewer creates montages of unspeakable originality, editing parallel transmissions into an individual blend. This art form is rhythmic, improvisational, and ironic. Cable stations that repeat movies several times a day actually allow viewers to see complete movies over the course of several days, but with the scenes "out of order." But who is to say, ultimately, what the correct order of those scenes is?

Channel flipping, still viewed as a behavioral aberration—a violation of the *intentions* of filmmakers and programmers—becomes the norm when viewed from the perspective of IN.S.OMNIA. Isn't it possible that the singular state an intent channel flipper falls into is not, as it is often described, evidence of a "short attention span," but, rather, of a new kind of attention? The qualities of this new attention would include irreverence, quick decision making, ability to identify the whole from the fragment, and an exquisite taste for juxtaposition. Not a bad starting list of skills if one happened to be faced, on a daily basis, with an overwhelming onslaught of information.

"Is there a male/female dynamic to the fact that certain kinds of attention are valued more than others?" asks in.s.omniac R-I-P.

I'm reading a newsletter article describing the busy life of a public-interest biologist. Under the photo of her and her daughter, the caption reads "On being Sally's mom: 'You learn to go instantaneously from drafting Congressional testimony to playing silly games in the bathtub'." When it happens at home people think of it as entertainment. "Juggling career and family" is a phrase still curiously applied uniquely to women. Excuse my rubber nose. At work, it's called "multitasking"—a highly valued skill. I'm wondering if women are the ones who introduced this skill into the workplace. How many balls do you have in the air? (IN.S.OMNIA 1992)

The actual practice of home TV use differs so radically from its usual description (passive consumption) that we ask if a new analysis shouldn't be made of an activity we think we already understand: the activity of reading.

In his essay "Lire: Esquisse socio-physiologique" ("Reading: A Socio-Physiological Sketch"), Georges Perec writes that he wants to see reading

. . . brought back to what it is in the first place, a precise activity of the body, bringing into play certain muscles, diverse postures, sequential decisions, choices of time, an ensemble of strategies inserted into the continuum of social life that add up to the fact that one doesn't read in just any manner, at any time, or in any place, even if one is content to read just anything. (Perec 1985, 111)

Perec's simple observations—lists of reading postures, of places where one reads while waiting (in lines, in waiting rooms)—surprise with the familiar. He recounts dining with friends at a regular haunt and watching another habitué, a noted philosopher, read as he ate: "a mouthful, a concept, a mouthful, a concept." "How is one to understand," he asks, "the effect of this double nourishment, how can one describe it, measure it?" (Perec 1985, 122).

What Perec points out is that a study of reading as activity reveals to us not things of which we are ignorant but, rather, things we are in the habit of ignoring.

Dear to all writers as the image of the obedient reader may be, a quick look into our hearts reveals an awful truth. One in.s.omniac left this confession.

▌2 1 f e b 8 6   f r o m   T h e   B a d   R e a d e r
I am the bad reader. O, writers! When the journalists ask you the question about your Ideal Reader it is me you are describing in reverse. Or you might say I am the worm in the apple of your mind's eye. Or you might skip to the beginning of the next paragraph.

Like I do. Frequently. Who wants to be read by a reader who jumps on the flaw in your first sentence, then jumps to conclusions, then jumps to the next entry. Who wants me?

IN.S.OMNIA is for the ideal reader with the ideal case of insomnia. I sleep long (and untroubled by a guilty conscience). My guilt disappeared when mere "bad habits" developed into obsessions.

I am the bulimic/anorexic/alcoholic of printed matter, sucking the chocolate off my fingertips that are covered with the feathers of my ripped down bathrobe.

In school we were taught to read almost as strictly as we were taught to write. Ma, a dog ate my report card on the way home.

Let me count the ways:

I slouch

I hold the book at a bad angle

I bend over the corners of the page instead of finding a bookmark

I set the book face down on the floor when I go to answer the phone

I do not turn on the light

I move my lips

I snap the binding by touching the front cover to the back

I rip out the whole page when the Xerox is broken

I prop it up against the butter dish and twirl spaghetti sauce on it

But these are merely violences against the object.

Hear how I harm the message:

It's a cute truism to cite how folks flip from back to front (holding a book in the right hand, riffling with the left thumb, standing under the fluorescents in a B. Daltons, a Waldenbooks).

21feb86 from The Bad Reader
What I do is more insidious: I skim FORWARD, mocking the intended order by a jerky, silent movie spoof of the readerly process. My skim implies to the author: you needn't have bothered with this bunch of pages here, this chapter over there.

My whole demeanor says: I can't be bothered to read this word-for-word. I'm after the gist, but not even your gist—MY gist, whatever gist I happen to find in the cursory glance I give your book.

I think I have read the last book I'll ever read. I mean, "read" the way one "should" read: slowly, respectfully, savoring every phrase, every word, naively—waiting to be surprised by the author even if what's to come is predictable, loving the book as a hunk of heart and craft, loving the author for having been such a wonderful person to have written it.

I think I read the last book I shall have ever read long ago, in my early twenties.

When I read now, I skim. What I want from a book is an idea of what it would be like to read it, if I had the time. I say: "I would recommend this book to a 20-year-old, to myself as a 20-year-old. I think I would like it."

Sometimes I don't even skim according to my own will. I will check a book out of the library and read only what a previous reader has underlined. I get an impression of a book, an impression of the mind of the previous reader, and an impression of what students think a University demands of them. But it's not reading. "Reading" as it "should" be.

I would rather "have read" than "read"; rather "write" than "read"; rather "have written" than "write." Let me have done with it.

I am not the reader I would like for my writing. I am the bad reader.
(IN.S.OMNIA)

Underlying nearly all contemporary discussion of literature is an unspoken agreement to imagine that books are read in silence, in sequence, and with full attention.

By contrast, IN.S.OMNIA acknowledges the flightiness of its users and shines the light of this experience on dark regions of the paper-and-ink world. In.s.omniacs realize that a page of a book is already the full equivalent of an electronic message—arbitrarily chopped, free to roam and recombine in the form of a photocopy. In.s.omniacs become aware of the juxtapositions in their own reading habits (a chapter of this, then a page of that, then an article from the paper). They understand that there is a tacit agreement between writer and reader to ignore the fact that books are written in small chunks over many days.

Certain realizations of this play of message linking—that is to say, certain families of computer programs—have come to be known as "hypertext." The best beginning definition of hypertext is that of Theodor H. Nelson who first put the term into circulation in the 1960s.

By "hypertext" I mean nonsequential writing—text that branches and allows choices to the reader, best read at an interactive screen. As popularly conceived, this is a series of text chunks connected by links which offer the reader different pathways. (Nelson cited in Landow 1992, 4)

Invisible Seattle's Novel Project was hypertext in a palpable way. Boxes containing scraps of paper linked by hand with scotch tape and retranscribed on word processors. But it shared with hypertext programming an acute, passionate, informal attitude toward text. It particularly opened the door for fervent sampling of the texts of history. The search for ever more astonishing juxtapositions leads users of hypertext into the obscurity of unpopular epochs and forgotten genres. Variant remixes of works exist happily side by side. It becomes harder to say when a hypertext is finished, or where one work leaves off and another begins. Projects that operate by linking are ephemeral enthusiasms that wane rather than organic works that come to closure.

The cultural world as formerly imagined was a manicured landscape of disciplines—music, literature, painting—and genres. Within these genres stood rows of monuments, each with its own gate, its own admission price. Respectful silence required. Over this calm cemetery has crashed a raucous wave of "information"—fact, fiction, history, current events, foaming in styles high-tech, low-brow, stone-age, and world-weary—breaking everything into pieces. This is the hilarious sea in which we now swim, grabbing handfuls of disparate beauty and squeezing them together to make new toys.

The period we are entering will be marked by the gradual recognition of everyday activities that function by linkage much more smoothly than IN.S.OMNIA. This period will see the ascendance of a new aesthetic animated by the vision of the cultural world as composed of mobile, *interchangeable* fragments—common property—messages constantly in motion, ready to be linked into new constellations. The system will be understood to operate more and more on the reader's terms, rather than the author's and publisher's.

The double nourishment of Perec's philosopher is a signpost to what may become a new kind of conscious enjoyment. Ongoing rooms on IN.S.OMNIA have recorded users' off-line combinations of experience: books and signs read from buses, sculpture viewed while listening to a Jack Benny show, music overheard while making love. In a de facto levelling gesture, these lists posit a *structural* equality between arts high and low, works canonical and crank.

The words will be forged to name and discriminate among these linked experiences. Apples will be flagrantly compared to oranges. A perfume, a broken muffler, the texture of a boot, two bird calls, and an electronic message will be understood to form an inseparable and organic whole.

exempli gratia vi

86feb01 from Multatuli
There is no talking about writing on this board. There is only writing.
We sit down and strike the keys, probably without moving our vocal
chords, and inscribe the light trace on the dark screen. First question:
Is some writing more privileged than other kinds? Are certain topics
inherently more real, more worthy of attention? Are certain genres (the
novel, fiction) inherently more noble than others? Second question:
How does writing advertise in what category it belongs? Words await us
on a page. Do they tell us "I am fiction" or "I am a novel" and, if so,
how? (IN.S.OMNIA)

Photos: Gyda Fosslanc

Lex Station Borges, an IN.S.OMNIA installation at Seattle's Henry Art Gallery August–September 1986. In.s.omniacs used the image of an arctic meteorological outpost to imagine an environment where the new genres of writing discovered on the electronic bulletin board system could take physical form. Instead of weather data, the "station" gathered creative messages from visitors. The geometrically expanding bookshelves await the chapters of the chain-letter novel, The Library of Borges.

The "Dear Diary" table of Lex Station Borges.

(In the "Successful Singles" Room)

▌86feb12 from Oncle Jean
Most men find it difficult to work for a female supervisor. Perhaps this is why I have never married. The problem started in early childhood. All children should have some form of religious instruction, but neither my parents nor my teachers gave me any. When I think back on my upbringing. . . . Boy, I would enjoy going back and telling off some of my high school teachers. Especially that Mr. Klingsor, in 11th grade chemistry. . . .▌

▌86feb21 from Interior Boy
Power and Sex, nothing else matters. I haven't been interested in anything but power and sex for years. My boss and I have a ho-hum relationship, a typical bondage/SM thing that's been going on for too long now. Most men find it difficult to work with a female supervisor. Not me—we've got a whole routine worked out, and it's smooth. We've set up a little chapel in the office. She dresses up like a nun, and I dress up like Buster Brown, and we do the communion service after work, only when it's over, I'm tied up and we're ready for "Catechism." The

catechism is brief—my boss says, "All children should have some form of religious instruction. Are you ready for today's lesson, Buster?" I always have an orgasm when she says that, but lately, it hasn't been the religious experience it used to be. It's more like work. I hate work. I hate learning. I hate school. I would enjoy going back and telling off some of my high school teachers. My boss used to teach high school. I had her for a teacher when I was in high school. She taught a course called "Power and Sex." For 12th graders. She had a routine where all the boys . . . ▌

▌8 6 f e b 2 6   f r o m   s t i c k   d o o d
The Philippine Quatrains
I
Marcos says: You men will see my male wisdom and come to thank me
 in Hell.
You like Cory now, but maternal care would soon make you despise her.
For your own good, I can't give in now, I might have saved face with
 Laurel;
Most men find it difficult to work with a female supervisor. . . .
V
Marcos's hold begins the day of Army induction
Most boys have to be cleansed of the leftist-Catholic rot
"All children should have some form of religious instruction"
Is a great thing to say if you want to get shot (IN.S.OMNIA)▌

Gyda Fossland

A visitor pauses to put pen to "Diary" and participate in a structured literary collaboration based on shared constraints.

Gyda Fossland

A device halfway between a phone booth and a confessional, the IN.S.OMNIUM public writing console was Lex Station Borges's experiment number 1. Coin-operated, IN.S.OMNIUM posits a genre of literary engagement limited only by time and spare change.

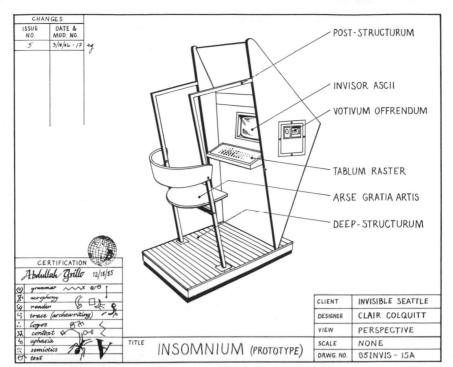

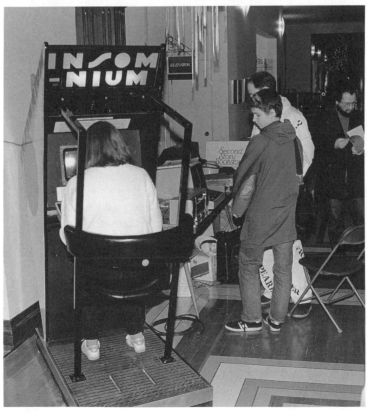

An IN.S.OMNIUM installed at Seattle's Wallingford Center, 1987.

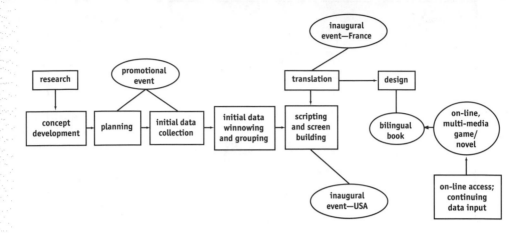

The ambitious mega-project Invisible America. *For those who write on the IN.S.OMNIA bulletin board, this unrealized plan is the best indicator of the spreading, ongoing shape of literary genres to come. Many of the sub-structures of* Invisible America *have been used to shape other projects.*

The man looked at us with sudden solemnity.

"Shall we begin?"

He broke the seal on the envelope, extracted a document, and read aloud.

"I, Cyrus T. Fielding . . . "

All present gasped.

Who in the Western Hemisphere had not been soaked by a cloudburst of obituaries of Cyrus T. Fielding in the past week? Who could have been unaware of his huge fortune, his resolute oddity, his fantastic mansion, his passion for the works of Jules Verne that had led him not only to amass the largest collection of manuscripts and first editions outside of France but also to design and have built in 1958 a gigantic plywood submarine, the *Nautilus,* which, on its unique voyage (thankfully unmanned) corkscrewed to an unknown depth beneath the mud of Lake Washington?

**". . . being of sound mind and body hereby call upon IN.S.OMNIA . . . "
the hearty voice continued, speaking aloud for the first time the essential ideas of what has become the project called *Invisible America.***

A codicil to Fielding's will—for that is what was being read that night before our demicredulous ears—charged IN.S.OMNIA with a project whose aspirations and seeming impossibility couldn't fail to captivate us.

Fielding proposed a variation on a theme by Jules Verne, to be based on a novel of 1899 entitled *Le Testament d'un Excentrique* (The Will of an Eccentric Millionaire). In the Verne novel a wealthy Chicagoan leaves his entire fortune to the winner of a board game (The Noble Game of Goose), a game played with the states of the U.S.A. substituted for the usual squares, a game in which the players, chosen at random from Chicago's citizenry, actually had to travel to the states indicated, dispersed to the corners of the country at the throw of the dice.

Verne had used the idea of those chance movements to make a methodical, guidebook-style description of the continental United States. We were to use our questionnaires and public diaries to make manifest the ignored and imaginative geography of an invisible America, written by its inhabitants, who best know its secrets!

Verne had produced a rollicking, traditional adventure novel. We were to produce a computer-based, interactive, electronic game/map/novel!

Verne had honored America with the attentions of his genius. We were to return the compliment by translating the game/novel, once completed, into French, and making it available via Minitel to the sporting readers of France!

You could say that *Invisible America* refutes the stultifying sameness of what is commonly produced under the name of fiction.

You could say that no new cultural vision of America has been presented since the 1950s, and that *Invisible America* is designed to supplant the worn-out myth of the white suburban postwar family with its eternally rebelling teens, disintegrating in the "modern" landscape of television, urban decay, and status symbols.

We prefer to say that we fell head-over-heels for the project put before us that night by the late Fielding's emissary. In fact, our talk became so intense that, much to our chagrin, we hadn't the opportunity to thank our visitor before he quietly packed up, donned his hat, and trotted off into the night.

Since then each of us has had a single-minded desire to play this game to take this voyage. And as the field does not yet exist, it is up to us to build it. (*IN.S.OMNIA Print Outs 1* 1987, 1)

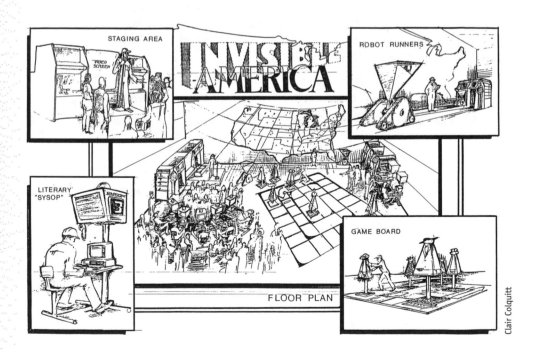

Clair Colquitt

Possible Goals for an Electronic Encyclopedia

1. Tell the whole Truth about everything, and list it alphabetically.

2. Tell a number of intertwined fictional stories about characters drawn from every possible social and cultural background that represents the whole world, and list them alphabetically.

3. Under the guise of telling a parodic "Truth" about everything, compile an accurate anthology of the thought of one's time, and list it alphabetically.

4. Under the guise of telling stories, present the tools of storytelling as emblems of the desire to believe in a (nonexistent) "everything" and a (nonexistent) "thought of one's time," and list them alphabetically.

5. Provide a space for the pursuit of all of the above. Furnish it with parks, bedrooms, coffeehouses, exhibition halls, recliner chairs, conference tables, and list the traces of its use alphabetically. (*IN.S.OMNIA Print Outs 2* 1987, 38)

From Messages to Projects: New Genres for a New Geography

"I spent last night in Missouri, Rhode Island, and California! And I won this beautiful ashtray!" So begins a sample advertisement for the dial-up, "publication" phase of the project *Invisible America*.

How about you?

You're overdue for a vacation!

INVISIBLE AMERICA

is more than a computer game, more than a novel . . .

It's the most stupendous literary event of the last 320 years!

Gorgeous scenery, breathtaking danger, tacky souvenirs!

A test-tube novel—literature by artificial dissemination.

Travel a computer landscape fraught with arcane knowledge, scenic oversights, and gossip to make you blush beet red—all written by the people who live there!

INVISIBLE AMERICA

The hottest game/novel in town! (*IN.S.OMNIA Print Outs 1* 1987, 91)

What on earth is a "game/novel?" Why does it need a slash down its center? This hybrid makes a convenient doorway to the issue of genre and form via a survey of IN.S.OMNIA forms.

The Plan for Invisible America, from which the ad above is culled, is riddled with slashes and hyphens, like most of the texts that try to articulate the growing complexities of cultural production. Genre benders such as performance/installation, video/environment, and the ubiquitous grab-bag "multimedia" (which evolved past its hyphen into a single word in the late 1980s) are evidence of the wanton recouplings—linkages—of genres loosed from their familiar moorings.

It is an injustice to describe the Novel Project as simply a "novel," first because no single version of the text can claim priority over other existing versions (or the myriad of potential versions still waiting to be compiled), and second, because this leaves out the questionnaires, posters, performances, street encounters, and sculptural installations that deserve (and received) every bit as much attention as the book from their audience.

Why call a novel a novel, a poem a poem? To place a text within a tradition, is one answer. To facilitate direct comparison of a text with others of its kind, or to signal to a potential purchaser of a magazine or book the nature of its contents, or to deny the literal truth of the accounts a text contains—these are other possibilities.

The well-stocked *wunderkammer* around us assure us that generic names are not needed for hybrid creations to reach an audience thirsty for interesting work.

Of greater interest is the light the small efforts of IN.S.OMNIA may shed on the larger and more important forms of creativity around us. The size and mechanisms of these ubiquitous creations are still hidden under a patchwork of old labels. A transitional expression such as "hypertext novel," for example, will soon be seen as a contradiction in terms. Accurate names may eventually help us see accurately.

So—what to call the new shapes of work on IN.S.OMNIA? As we've seen with the novel of Seattle, policing the formal borders and declaring works "complete" and "finished" is problematic. For the time being we have come to call just about everything a "project." Project with the accent on the Greek prefix *pro-* —that which comes before, that which is planned in advance with no worry about its completion, that which is potential—"project" as in a design on the future.

IN.S.OMNIA's partitions, we'll remember, are called rooms, and over the years these rooms have tended to migrate into certain generic categories.

"Conversation rooms" are the historic source of electronic bulletin boards. Rhetorically they tend to mimic spoken exchange and are most often shaped into club-meeting or reading-group formats with room names such as "Derrida," "CI-NE-MA" (film theory), "Faulkner," "Vlad's Pad" (Nabokov), and "Tristram's Shanty" (Sterne).

"Travesty-of-Print rooms" overtly mimic printed genres, often with such self-explanatory names as "Letters to the Editor," "Dear Abby," and "Reporters at Large." This category includes the single-user serial stories that one suspects were written as paper works first rather than composed expressly for the bulletin board. Although the chosen travesty format tends to predict the style in these rooms, the estrangement of the medium still encourages messages to rebel and explore. One brief attempt to regularize IN.S.OMNIA's functions on the model of a print magazine (rooms called "Contents," "Columns," "Features," "Reviews," and the like) was answered with the mysterious appearance of rooms called "Mailing Wrapper," "Staples," "Page Numbers," "Perfume Sample," and "Blow Card" (the annoying, loose, subscription cards placed between pages).

"Investigation rooms," such as the "Naive Writing Room" discussed earlier, begin to adapt themselves consciously to the thirst for surprise that eventually overtakes most rooms, whatever their first intent. The spirit of these rooms was summarized by one of their leading users.

▮92mar03 from Grothus
Every time I walk into a library I am a Livingstone or an Amundsen. Every time I pick up a scrap of paper off the sidewalk I am a Darwin collecting another species to fit into my theoretical paradigm. On IN.S.OMNIA we share our finds with our colleagues: we display fossil texts in the museum and debate their various meanings in the club.

1. transforming data into information

2. transforming information into information

3. building and using machinery to facilitate quicker transformation of data and information (IN.S.OMNIA)▮

"Greetings to my fellow literary sinners!" began Harry Mathews, at the start of a suite of messages left on IN.S.OMNIA in 1985. He was entering into the thriving "Literary Sins" room, a prime example of the category of rooms that could be called "Workshops."

In these "Workshop rooms" Oulipean and Oulipo-inspired formal procedures are tried and evaluated. Mathews's contribution is indicative of the kinds of structured work done over the years in rooms such as "Art A to Z," "1–10," and "Successful Singles."

For your amusement and perhaps use, I propose this contribution to the means available to you in the cultivation of vice—a procedure that will enable you to imitate as closely as you like any prose writer you choose. The procedure has a

name, not necessarily definitive but handily abbreviated: the Mathews Perfectible Parody & Pastiche Procedure: PPPP.

PPPP = the combination of three subsidiary procedures:

1. Homosyntaxism, an Oulipean method introduced by Noel Arnaud (for verification see *La Littérature Potentielle*)

2. Transplant, an invention of HM which might here by analogy be dubbed homolexicalism

3. Choice of subject

Through a systematic recycling of vocabulary and selection of text from within an oeuvre "a new text typical of the author is virtually guaranteed."

A final word: in poetry, PPPP "works," but not in the same way, or at least not usually. The results it produces read like the work of someone who never was, perhaps a mystical marriage of you and the author you have chosen. In other words, they are unexpectedly original, although it's hard to say to whom the originality belongs. You might as well take the credit. (IN.S.OMNIA 1985)

The PPPP went on to produce some extraordinarily sinful pastiches and parodies, and its use continues to be suspected whenever a particularly "familiar" stylistic note is struck on the bulletin board.

"Successful Singles" began when in.s.omniac Oncle Jean came upon, and entered, a questionnaire from a singles dating service that rated compatibility by reactions to a series of statements such as "most men find it difficult to work with a female supervisor," "all children should have some form of religious instruction," "I would enjoy going back and telling off some of my high school teachers," "male strip shows should be illegal," and so on. The challenge Oncle Jean set for in.s.omniacs was to write texts that included, in some plausible rubric, all the questionnaire's statements verbatim, and in the order listed.

The effect of the accumulating "Successful Singles" entries, when read together, was eerie—an encantatory suite that begged to be considered as a whole work.

This consideration of the totality of the "Successful Singles" room was an important bridge to the era of attempts to combine multiple constraints, multiple concerns, into plans for IN.S.OMNIA writing that for the first time truly deserved the name "projects." These projects, like the multiple-constraint paper books of Oulipeans Mathews, Perec,

Calvino, and others, emerged from the variety of activities of the bulletin board to be considered IN.S.OMNIA's feature attractions.

A message from this period sets out some basic principles of "project" construction.

▌8 6 j u n 2 0   f r o m   M u l t a t u l i
Another good project idea is *Sentimental Voyage Sentimentale*. By good I mean complete and multifaceted.

1. There is an ur-text. Laurence Sterne's account of his trip to France, *Sentimental Journey*, which serves as an invisible guide. (Fact about the history of literature: Most new texts are rewritings or arguments with other texts. *Don Quixote* address-es itself to *Amadis of Gaul*; *Ulysses* borrows the structure of the *Odyssey*, etc.)

2. There is a "genre" to play with—The Travel Diary. Production of short, dated entries. A page or two pages at a time to be combined in various ways.

3. There is a method, or at least the glimmerings of one. The entire text will be somehow and expansion of the words "voyage" and "sentimental," which are nearly the same in English and in French. So we begin by collecting "senti-ments," "sentimental places," "sentimental encounters, etc." until soon we have assembled a large palette of elements to be included in each dated entry.

4. There is a "focus of investigation." Namely, the intersection of language and geography. We are producing a bilingual text collaborating via telecommunica-tions with French writers. We are shuttling back and forth between two cities using language as the communicating vessel. For here is the notion that makes this a super idea. Each group of writers (French and American) collects proper names. There's a Bon Marché store in Seattle and one in Paris. A "New York Deli" in Paris, and one in Seattle. So whenever the narrator in Paris (writing in French) steps into one of these places, he/she emerges from the corresponding place in Seattle writing in English. The PROPER NOUN is the door between cities and lan-guages and controls the oscillation of the text.

5. Derrida has noted that the PROPER NOUN is a key to the theory and history of writing. It was the key to decipherment of hieroglyphics (translation, cross-cul-tural passage) since the only way to represent a foreign name was phonetic. (IN.S.OMNIA)▌

How can we choose from among the many projects formulated just a few that will indicate their scope and flavor?

There is *OK Corral* (IN.S.OMNIA 1985), which plots to have contributors variously rescript the famous wild western shootout of the same name, while using as many acronyms (of the "OK" variety) as possible, and meditating on the successive waves of mythologizing worked on this historical event by Hollywood.

There is *Miss Scarlet's Letter* (IN.S.OMNIA 1986), which has the goal of reformulating Margaret Mitchell's *Gone with the Wind* by adding to it the astringent of *The Scarlet Letter* and exposing it to the light of actual, well-researched history of the Civil War. In.s.omniacs became Civil War buffs, stocking the room with bibliographies, while the fortuitous arrival, in another room, of an English composition book on sentence structure completed the basic ingredients. A particular sentence structure, and it alone, is to be used for each successive chapter.

There is the mighty *Constitutions Unlimited* (IN.S.OMNIA 1988), which posits the existence of a chain of franchise stores that sell constitutions written to order. The legal eagerness of litigation-happy American culture is examined in a project that envisions as its public form a printed book—a facsimile of the binders full of documents given to new franchisees by the corporate headquarters—replete with blank forms, office procedures, and the proprietary secret formula to constitutional composition, itself a massive Oulipean machine.

Ultimately, however, even looking at these complex "projects" may mask the structural significance of what occurs on IN.S.OMNIA. All of the projects wax and wane alongside one another, affecting one another, infecting one another. In a sense it is all one piece, but a piece that no longer can be compared to a book. It is a library. A library, as in.s.omniac Strange Justice put it, "from a Warner Brothers cartoon, a library after closing hours, left to its own devices, a library where books begin to sing and dance, where the card catalogue becomes an accordion and the microfiches dance with the rubber stamps" (IN.S.OMNIA 1990).

It is just this sort of vision that frightens many who recognize, quite rightly, that The Library (that ancient architectural metaphor for the organization of knowledge) is coming apart at the seams.

"I also had the misfortune of following Nicholas Vroman, whose brilliant paper ("Destruction of the Library") had provoked Di Giovanni to a spirited debate in which the name of Borges figured several times." This passage from the first chapter of the IN.S.OMNIA chain letter novel project, *The Library of Borges* (*IN.S.OMNIA Print Outs 4* [1986] 1990, 3), sets out the issues.

Vroman's general argument was as entertaining as it was fallacious. The Library, he asserted, was no longer threatened by the Huns or the Mongols, but by the very books it sought to preserve, by the very writing it was supposed to contain. Certain artists had recently devised books glued permanently shut or covered in concrete, books composed of blank pages waiting for the reader's pen to complete them, books consisting of words on photographic paper that disappear forever the first time the pages are opened—monstrous books, in short, that refuse to be merely containers for writing but boldly assert their bookness and defy the miracle of xerox or the labors of the copyist. The writing formerly entrusted to books had now returned to its origins on walls or tablets—or fled to a future of ephemeral green screens disrupting what he first termed the "marriage of convenience" (what he later denounced as "that spurious cohabitation") between Writing and The Book. To maintain that any surface can provide a support for writing is potentially to admit any object into The Library. He cited an unemployed Moroccan gardener (Abdellah Grillo) who wandered the city of Fez covering walls, trees, rocks, even the insides of library books with a delirious calligraphy of his own invention—it was as if the entire city was a series of blank pages bound into a comprehensive but invisible book by the gardener's graphomania. No library could devise a single criterion for including such an aberration; none could justify excluding it. No longer able to impose an ordering principle on the chaos of experience, it has become that chaos—an arbitrary or willfully incomplete collection of heterogeneous objects. The physical library—the stone façade, the Corinthian capitals—will, of course, remain; its conceptual site will soon be entirely destroyed.

Di Giovanni offered the following refutation: Borges took pleasure in hypothesizing impossible books—for example, the apocryphal Chinese novel, *El jardín de los senderos que se bifurcan,* but only as a way of defining the limits of The Library. To write such a novel that would include all forks of a continuously bifurcating narrative is conceivable (and certainly not beyond the powers of, say, a Borges or a Herman Wouk); to imagine a reader for it is impossible. Such is also the case for certain of the aberrations cited by Vroman (no one can decipher the gardener's invented writing, no eye can read a book that refuses to open). Thus, the problem of excluding them can be resolved definitively and The Library is vindicated. What constitutes The Library is not a particular class of physical objects (book, stone, or CRT screen); what matters is that whatever is inside it can be read.

Time cut short this lively session. Most of the auditors retired to the hotel bar where Vroman extended the debate by postulating a new kind of reader; a polite few remained to hear my description of the storage potential of CD-ROM disks.

A recurring fear in the wake of this debate is that the disintegration of libraries into messages will lead to a kind of desert of minimalist monads—all fragmentary, all out of context—a world of sound bites and slogans. But this fear would appear to be put to rest by the experiences of IN.S.OMNIA. As we have seen, fragmented genres are only too eager to glom on to others and form constellations, to form projects. In.s.omniac aesthetics hold that depth and richness can't be achieved in any single work but only by users' placing the work in constellation with others.

If a drastic restructuring of text can be intimated on a system as homespun as IN.S.OMNIA, what is the shape of projects on a single, *powerful,* medium—hypertext programs such as Eastgate Systems's Storyspace or the Internet's World Wide Web?

Much of the consideration currently focused on hypertext concerns the notion of an "interactive" text. The most curious aspect of this "new development" is the picture it paints of the earlier, "noninteractive" text.

A work that allows its reader to jump from section to section by choice clearly shares this characteristic with existing paper reference books. In fact, as we saw earlier, books have always secretly been used in this interactive way. In its discussion of interactivity, *The Plan for Invisible America* asks,

> **Aren't these works (even allowing for such typical computer adventure game possibilities as picking up and putting down items at the player's discretion) still deeply conservative? Conservative in the sense that the expert/artist conserves approximately 95% control of the final experience.**

A speculative scale of literary activities that demonstrate more interactivity follows.

> **. . . improvisational theater sketches where the themes are given by the audience; workshop situations where the production is animated by a teacher; ghost writer arrangements; interviews.**

> **At the extreme end of interactivity would be a kind of artwork modeled on the structure of psychological counseling. In it the "author's" task would be to encourage and assist an individual "reader" in the composition of her or his own text. The author's responsibilities would include making coffee and massaging the reader's neck.**

> **Real interactivity doesn't begin until the user has the power to do something with the text that the author doesn't like. (*IN.S.OMNIA Print Outs 1* 1987, 114)**

But in the shadows of the many topical uses of hypertext, waiting for the right technical boiling point, we discern the presence of the master project of the European Enlightenment, the *Encyclopedia* of Diderot and d'Alembert.

Historian Robert Darnton describes the efforts of one of the principal Enlightenment publishers to assemble an all-inclusive encyclopedia. "He divided the cognitive universe into its constituent parts—at first twenty branches of knowledge, twenty-six by the time he issued the prospectus, and eventually more than fifty . . . then he hired several persons to cut apart two sets of the original *Encyclopédie* and the *Supplement* and to file each article under one of the twenty-six rubrics" (Darnton 1979, 421).

If only the linkage problem could be solved, the encyclopedists must have thought, universal knowledge would lie at our fingertips. The temptations to refer to hypertext in totalizing and universalizing terms seem to be great. Dreams are sketched in terms of universal access from anywhere to any computers—the whole history of writing at your fingertips. The system that hypertext's namer, Theodor Nelson envisions, dubbed Xanadu "provides A UNIVERSAL DATA STRUCTURE TO WHICH ALL OTHER DATA MAY BE MAPPED" (emphasis Nelson's) (Nelson in Bolter, 1991, 102).

Nelson's vision is predicated on his data typing and marking system becoming universally adopted. But there are bound to be data that will refuse to be typed and marked correctly, for reasons of economic competition if nothing else. It's the "nature" of data, the nature of messages. IN.S.OMNIA has shown us that hypertext tends to escape the intent of its creators.

But what other visions for the encyclopedic project are there? The short essay *Prospectus for &ncyclopedia 1* (*IN.S.OMNIA Print Outs 2* 1987) takes another tack. Just as cities begin to mature once buildings are put into their second and third uses, literary forms such as the encyclopedia mature as their original inhabitants leave and parodists arrive to rebuild and reorient them.

The *Prospectus* lays out a few characteristics of their "dream system."

The disappointing thing about many information data bases is that they give you the information you want quickly, accurately, and efficiently.

Paper reference books, on the other hand, require you to do a considerable amount of wandering and perusing before you find the desired entry.

I could see an electronic system of alphabetic consultation that deposits you

NEAR the entry you want, like at the closest subway station. How far will you have to walk? A neighborhood you don't know. Strangely quiet. A woman startles you by asking if you'll please hold her child while she gets the wheel of the stroller fixed. "I'll be back in five minutes," she says. "But," you object as she recedes, " . . . my research . . . urgent. . . ."

Above all, the *Prospectus* seeks to apply to the Encyclopedic project an irrecuperable irreverence that resembles the affectionate, if rough, handling musical samples get at the hands of hip-hop remixers.

Writing on electronic systems is beginning to struggle, seriously, to its feet. It's time for us to do for hypertext what *Tristram Shandy* did for the then-young novel: grab the rug, yank, and trip it! (*IN.S.OMNIA Print Outs 2* 1987, 8)

Most contemporary worries about the changes wrought by the message linking mentality in general, and hypertext in particular, are based on the vision one-for-one substitution of hypertext for the book.

Far more likely than this is a scenario in which some *combination* of books and hypertext is used, some constellation of media that allows for varied modes of participation. For isn't the assumed self-sufficiency of books itself illusory? Don't books already, viewed with a linking mentality, interpenetrate one another? Don't dictionaries, to choose only the most literal example, have a right to invade any other book with which they share words?

In 1986 the in.s.omniacs dreamed up a media constellation after accepting an invitation from the University of Washington's Henry Art Gallery to participate in a show titled "15th Avenue Studio: Artists and Process." The result was *LEX Station Borges*, a "Literary Experiment Station" that took as its conceptual model an arctic meteorological outpost and contained instruments designed to see which way the lexical winds were blowing.

The installation featured the unveiling of the first IN.S.OMNIUM. The IN.S.OMNIUM, described as a device "halfway between a phone booth and a confessional," was a former video game that had been converted into a public writing receptacle (coin-operated, of course) by Clair Colquitt. Callers were linked automatically to the bulletin board and participated in the current slate of projects.

In addition to this centerpiece, *LEX Station Borges* offered a homey little table with an open diary and an invitation to "add to an intimate autobiography." A wall became the collection point of "The Dead Sea Scrawls," a memorial to dead or dying languages. "Palimpsestia/Humumentia" was a bookshelf stocked not only with books, but pens, erasers, and white paint. An homage to Tom Phillips's altered Victorian novel, *A Humument* (1980), this was a temptation to the forbidden, to "rewrite these books."

The "Reference Desk" carried forward the data base concepts of the Novel Project, reaping "the raw materials of literature: definitions, descriptions, locutions." It also provided a key idea for *Invisible America*: the compilation of an *Atlas*.

But the most provocative data-gathering device in the LEX Station was a realization of Borges's story, "The Garden of Forking Paths" (Borges 1962, 19). Visitors found the first chapter and a set of instructions for a chain-letter novel called *The Library of Borges*. Chapters were to be sent from writer to writer, each chapter producing two alternative continuations. This set in motion "a work eternally in progress, with versions in French, Spanish, German multiplying around the globe, posing, in subject and form, questions about the nature of the book, the library."

Lex Station Borges was, in a sense, an attempt to give a physical form to the experience of IN.S.OMNIA. A small studio equipped with multiple chairs, multiple methods of inscription invited users to sit elbow to elbow to read and write on different projects. The discrete projects somehow added up to one big project.

But just how big can a "project" get, especially once it expands into multiple media?

The Plan for Invisible America (*IN.S.OMNIA Print Outs 2* 1987) was designed to answer this question. Compiled in 1987 as a report to IN.S.OMNIA, the mission of the *Plan* was to combine the worldview of the invisibles with nearly five years of genre-smashing experience on IN.S.OMNIA. And, true to the invisible policy that theory is most fruitfully discussed in the throes of an actual creative dilemma, it was not to be abstract or generic.

The *Plan* was to describe a single, hyperbolic "project" for which only the very sky was the limit. It was to have an ur-text for structure and historical resonance, a zone of investigation (geographic), and numerous frameworks for collaboration.

Despite the Cecil B. DeMille scale, the resulting document was expected to be thoroughly researched, with every step of its baroque process logistically sound, and every cent of the million-dollar hardware, software, and salary budget accounted for. *Invisible America*, the reasoning ran, must be a freeze-dried project, ready to go at a moment's notice—"just add hot boiling money." In the meantime, *Invisible America* could be scavenged for parts and provide inspiration for more immediately realizable projects.

From the fictional frame-tale of the millionaire's will that inspires the project to the bottom line, *The Plan for Invisible America* lays out a remapped vision of literary activity.

First, it presents three years' worth of diverse activities and events—research, translation, writing, programming, publicity, performance—as equal parts of the same project. There is a book in the mix, but it is only a small element. Then it shows how the project interacts with different sectors of its audience in different ways: encouraging them to be authors, game players, and spectators.

Finally, it sketches the outlines of a graphic "playing field" in which the game/novel grows through the contributions of both authors and players. The field—a single visual/verbal surface over which the screen of the electronic terminal "slides" in a continual bird's eye view—is a concrete alternative to interfaces that equate the screen to the page and are still conceptually bound to the book.

If the *Plan* is an incitement to anything, it is an incitement to dream confidently that sprawling projects can be as important to the culture as our favorite books are. Accomplishing that goal demands the eminently literary skills of scholarship and wit.

Who knows what further, more complex, constellations of form will result when projects such as *Invisible America* begin to unfurl into the hands of users.

Look what has happened to the black wall of the Vietnam Memorial in Washington, D.C. Viewed by traditional art critics it is nothing more than a closed, single artwork—a sculpture—by a single artist. Viewed from the perspective of IN.S.OMNIA it is a complex, still-developing project that involves all the traditions that users have built around it: paper rubbings, photography, ceremonies, and personal tokens. Embracing contradiction, the Vietnam wall project also absorbs the traditional, figurative sculpture of soldiers nearby that conservative groups put up as a response and protest to it. And beyond its purely visual-art aspects, The Vietnam Memorial is also a literary project. Its literature has not only been left in large quantities at the wall, but also it has been collected and published. In 1992 a play opened based on that writing. The tendrils of the project wind on and on, finding different audiences.

Many projects of similar structure are already under way. But few of them operate under a self-consciously "literary" banner. One of the best examples is the Dallas-based Church of the Subgenius. Much to the credit of its founding Popes and Reverends, it eschews almost entirely any literary claims. The formal coherence of its constellation of interactive performances ("devivals"), books ("sacred texts"), and its explosion of participatory graphic arts is expressed quite simply in its organizational metaphor. It is not a series of "art events," it is, quite simply, a church and fulfills the full slate of churchly functions.

What about these forms corresponds to the concealed creative "projects" under way in the culture at large? Time and again we see the pattern of an existing set of materials that are unlinked from their present context and relinked into a new form, *while staying in the same place*. A passionate pastime provides a conceptual pattern for understanding this restructuring.

Rotisserie league (also called "fantasy league") baseball is a pursuit in which groups of friends gather before the start of the major league baseball season and "draft" the names of real major league players from various real teams, which they then assemble into their own personal, "virtual" teams. These virtual teams prosper or fail according to the daily real-life exploits of their recombination of players, as followed in a given newspaper. Players who squander outstanding personal achievement in the ranks of feckless real teams may well take one of these virtual teams to glory in a rotisserie league World Series.

Rotisserie league baseball is not a world apart from Major League baseball—it is not a reflection or imitation—but rather is an *alternate use* of Major League baseball, with which it coexists and which it interpenetrates.

The same can be said of participants in the projects described above, each of whom *makes* of the existing elements a new combination, each of whom adapts its elements, and creates new ones as needed, to form a private, virtual version.

Once this rotisserie league structure is understood, isn't it possible that the traditional practices of attending college, and even reading, can be seen to operate in the same way? Because the changes we're discussing—we say it again—are not caused by, or even concerned with particular technologies but consist of an awareness of the real but invisible usage systems being applied to all technologies.

One of the most sublime formal constructs of IN.S.OMNIA was the result of a contact made in the wake of the Novel Project. Through friends of friends, the in.s.omniacs began to correspond with French writer Didier Coffy. Like the invisibles, Coffy was impassioned by the structural and algorithmic aspect of literature and by the formal allure of mapping. To this he added the methodical self-archaeology of Proust and Joyce, and a reverence for Naive Art in the *Art Brut* formulation of Jean Dubuffet. An offhand invitation to Coffy to draft for IN.S.OMNIA a description of Seattle (which Coffy had never seen) grew a massive, single-minded project that, according to Coffy's plans will call for him to be generating pages steadily until the year 2025 (Coffy 1985). The title of Coffy's giant work? *Invisible Seattle*!

More important than the similarities of the French *Invisible Seattle* to its American counterpart are the differences, not only of language but also of means, methods, and goals. We have here two alternate, completely different mappings of the same city. It's perfect, it's hilarious: two ambitious megaprojects with the same name. It's beside the point to try to group them as parts of the same project or organization or to trace linear genealogies between them. In a way that speaks volumes about the genres of the future, *Invisible Seattle* and *Invisible Seattle* are rotisserie leagues of each other, neither more real, neither primary.

exempli gratia vii

Invisible America
More Than a Game—More Than a Novel
And YOU may already be an author!

—Can you describe this Leprechaun?

—Can you remember the last time the weather was this bad?

—Can you sum up the faults of your local politicians in a single joke?

OF COURSE YOU CAN.

That's why you're ready to participate in the

MOST COLOSSAL LITERARY FEAT EVER ATTEMPTED:

"The description of a place by people who actually know something about it!"

The Place: Your part of America

The Author: You

We are assembling a gigantic, computer-based game/novel that will allow its player/readers to travel across a literary gameboard of the United States, filled with descriptions, hot tips, details, anecdotes, documents, narrow escapes, and romantic tirades, all written by the residents of the areas where the action takes place!

WHO KNOWS BETTER THAN YOU

—How to misbehave in order to attract the maximum local media coverage

—Where to hide a circus

—Whom to bribe to build a convention center

—Where the worst accidents happen and why

What would your state's seal look like if it really symbolized your state?

What are the Ten Unwritten Rules for surviving at your job?

Tell someone how to have the worst night of their life in your area.

An unexpected guest arrived at your place last night. You have to leave early and won't be back until late. Write this guest a note explaining what to fix for breakfast, how to use the shower, where to go sightseeing in the neighborhood, etc.

Draw a map of where a woman can't go alone at night.

I want to look like I belong here. What should I do?

What are the tell-tale signs that I have been here too long?

What should be carved above the door to your town hall?

What should be spraypainted above the door to your town hall?

Write a **TYPICAL** local newspaper story from your area. Be sure to include all the clichés. (*IN.S.OMNIA Print Outs 1* 1987, 35)

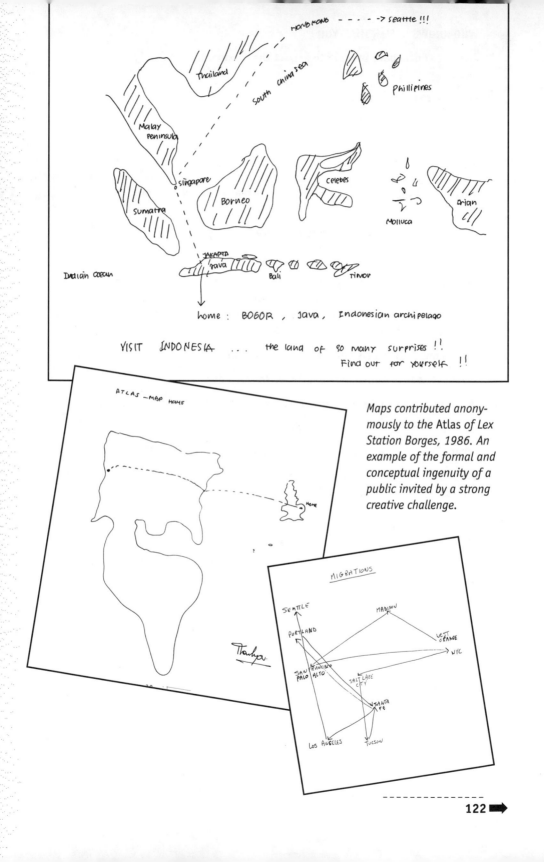

Thailand

HONG KONG - - - - -> seattle !!!

South china sea

Phillipines

Malay
Peninsula

singapore

Celebes

Borneo

Arian

sumatra

Molluca

JAKARTA
Java

Indian ocean

Bali

Timor

home : BOGOR , Java , Indonesian archipelago

VISIT INDONESIA ... the land of so many surprises !!
Find out for yourself !!

ATLAS — MAP HOME

HOME

Thanya.

MIGRATIONS

SEATTLE

MADISON

PORTLAND

WEST
ORANGE

NYC

SAN FRANCISCO
PALO ALTO

SALT LAKE
CITY

SANTA
FE

LOS ANGELES

TUCSON

Maps contributed anony-
mously to the Atlas of Lex
Station Borges, 1986. An
example of the formal and
conceptual ingenuity of a
public invited by a strong
creative challenge.

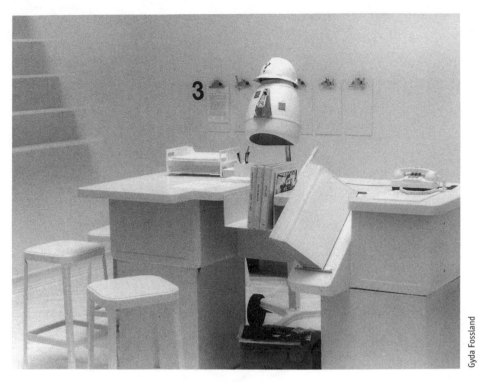

Lex Station Borges: the desk where the Atlas *was collected.*

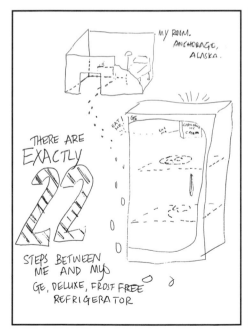

MY ROOM.
ANCHORAGE,
ALASKA.

THERE ARE
EXACTLY
22
STEPS BETWEEN
ME AND MY
GE, DELUXE, FROST FREE
REFRIGERATOR

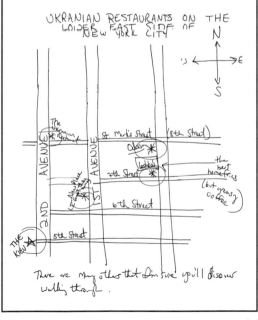

UKRANIAN RESTAURANTS ON THE
LOWER EAST SIDE OF
NEW YORK CITY

There are many others that I'm sure you'll discover
walking through.

AMERICAN LEAGUE ROSTER

Teams: 1 2 3 4 5 6 7 8 9 10 11 etc.

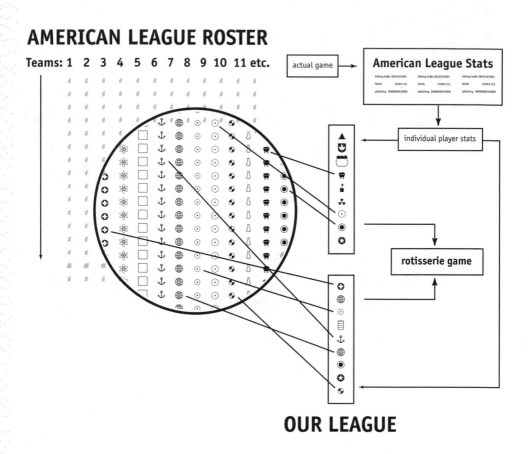

OUR LEAGUE

The relationship of the user to the given materials (teams, players) in rotisserie league baseball.

LIBRARIES AND BOOKSTORES

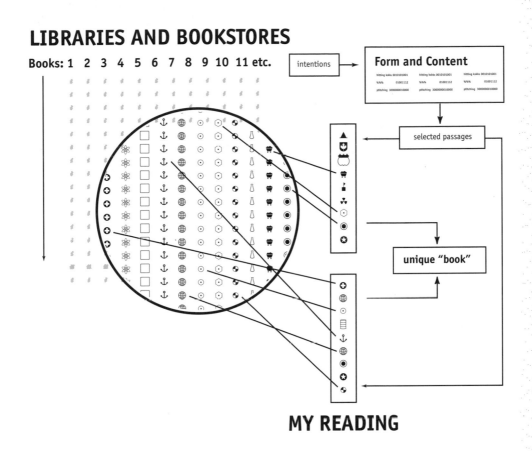

MY READING

The relationship of the user to the given materials (form, content) in literature and related cultural productions.

chapter 7

Anyone Can Play, Pro or Am: Tapping Everyday Creativity

A love of passionate, public discussion set the tone for early Invisible Seattle. "Wanted:" Read a 1980 handbill hung on telephone poles, "artists, poets, actors, dancers, architects, idle men, fallen women, all persons of slender means, dubious antecedents, and questionable loyalties."

VIS the Invisible

EFF the Ineffable

VOC the Invocable

How to Apply:

1. Appear at the Elliott Bay Café on any Monday after 8:00 P.M., and bring evidence of poor character.

2. You will find us conversing at the long table in the back.

3. No, not there! The longest one.

4. Be seated, please.

5. Surprise us.

Imagination is the only stable currency. Invest in Invisible Seattle. (Invisible Seattle 1980a)

The benefits were immediate. A pair of Elliott Bay Café drop-ins contributed the concept and the drawing for the Art Buck. A dollar-bill-sized scrap of scrip, the Art Buck "redeemable for Art, Void without Face" (its central cameo had been outlined with a dotted line that the bearer was obligated to draw in) played a part in the first series of Bumbershoot events.

The Novel Project began with the idea of a book signing where everyone in attendance would be authorized to sign. It posed the dangerous question: What constitutes qualified authorship?

A simple line of reasoning emerged. Novels are considered to be anthologies of different voices, tours de force of ventriloquism by a lone writer. Wouldn't the contrasts stand a chance of being wider and richer if the different voices were actually written by different people?

This simple notion seemed not only interesting—a hypothesis worth testing—but also potentially a laugh riot. Throughout the Novel Project the basic gag of turning the solemn creative process inside out fueled the proceedings. "There are 60,000 words in the naked novel," ran the flyer "some of them may be yours!" (Invisible Seattle 1983b).

As it turned out, contributors shaped plot, defined characters, and provided rich details. In those passages that characterized the multivocality of the project—the great lists and catalogs—there was a wealth it was hard to imagine coming from a single author.

The books on Henderson King's shelf share one peculiar property. Every single one of them contains the word Seattle in its title.

This City, Seattle!

Seattle in Search of Itself

Seattle Tells All

Seattle Goes on a Holiday

Seattle, Come Home

When the Sun Shines in Seattle

Seattle: Brown Bags and Bright Lights

Seattle: Yesterday's City of the Future . . .

Seattle on My Back

Seattle: Butt of Many Jokes

Sherlock Holmes Visits Seattle

Eating is Believing: an Eater's Guide to Seattle's Great Inexpensive Restaurants and Dessert Places . . .

Seattle, Summer of Sin

Sex—Seattle Style

Palmistry Facts of Seattle

Seattle Aerobic Moods Primer

Seattle Unlimited

I'll Build A Stairway to Seattle

Sanitary Seattle . . . (Invisible Seattle 1987, 182)

The first years of IN.S.OMNIA only confirmed that an extraordinary creativity on the part of people who did not consider themselves writers could be tapped under the right conditions.

Only after the urgent requirements of these projects had been fulfilled did the invisible planners of *Invisible America* begin to inquire in a systematic way into just what type of creativity they were dealing with. Was there no name for it? How did it mesh with what we have been taught to recognize as artistry? It was important to know because the *Invisible America* project would be a gargantuan attempt to engage this energy.

Among the most useful studies was that of Michel de Certeau. The French historian's *The Practice of Everyday Life* sets out a view of everyday creativity that flies in the face of the common image of society receiving the products of mass production in a sheeplike trance of "mass consumption."

"This essay is part of a continuing investigation of the ways in which users—commonly assumed to be passive and guided by established rules—operate" (Certeau, 1984 xi).

De Certeau questions the kinds of research that are used to "prove" this supposed passivity. He asks whether the activity of people in relation to mass-produced products is *consumption* or *use*.

> **For example, the analysis of the images broadcast by television (representation) and of the time spent watching television (behavior) should be complemented by a study of what the cultural consumer "makes" or "does" during this time and with these images. The same goes for the use of urban space, the products purchased in the supermarket, the stories and legends distributed by the newspapers, and so on. (Certeau, 1984 xi)**

De Certeau makes a distinction between a kind of creativity practiced by those who have a clearly delimited space in which to work (studio, laboratory, notebook) and their own choice of materials, and a kind of creativity practiced by those who create with whatever materials and time are available. He asserts that situations that are viewed conventionally as points of mute consumption can actually be sites of *production*—of intelligent, satirical, moving recombination and mis-use of given elements.

This description matched the discoveries of the Novel Project and of the rotisserie league deployments of IN.S.OMNIA. If the cultural world consists of discrete fragments, or messages, then these messages are constantly undergoing recombination, parody, undermining, in conversations, notes, home-recorded cassettes. There is out there a universe of users linking and creating, pursuing their own invisible pleasures.

De Certeau's study helped make the setting of everyday creativity more visible, but it also made clear a still more unsettling problem.

By its structure, *Invisible America*, like IN.S.OMNIA, asserts that messages of lasting interest can be produced by people who are not career writers, who don't consider themselves writers at all.

Some moments of creativity are generally understood as such—writing a poem, putting paint to canvas, the tableaux of performance art. *Invisible America* proposed to incorporate them side by side with the type of creativity found in fax machine gags, binder-cover drawings, and the tableaux of elaborate practical jokes. As in.s.omniac Strange Justice put it, "I no longer see any difference between the verbal hi-jinx of the novel I'm reading and the verbal hi-jinx of the passersby I listen to as I read. I tip my hat to the successful perpetrators of both" (IN.S.OMNIA 1991).

"What we've got here is a democratic view and an aristocratic view." In.s.omniac Multatuli indicated the core issue: "I love the fact that the board is open to all and that I can be astonished by anyone's writing. At the same time I recognize a part of myself that wants to identify the BEST users and be interested in what THEY are writing. I'm torn, I have one foot in each world" (IN.S.OMNIA 1992).

What is the difference between career (or "professional," or "vocational") writers and occasional (or "dilettante," or "Sunday") writers?

To ask that question brings us face-to-face with a list of attributes that is assumed but rarely spoken. Career writers of the Romantic/Modernist variety are thought to be unusually talented, most probably gifted with some kind of external inspiration, and of superior, even supernatural vision. Their authority is political, viz. Shelley's "Poets are the unacknowledged legislators of the world."

What emerges from IN.S.OMNIA is an invitation to dissociate the quality of the work from the qualities of the person who makes it. Or at least to say that the relationship of the person to the work is much more complex than "geniuses do good stuff."

Instead, a network of conditions appear—ability, mood, opportunity, challenge, materials—that can coalesce in a number of ways to produce quality work.

De Certeau, in order to get at the root of the almost willful blindness to everyday creativity, takes a long, hard look at the history of how sociologists, psychologists, and other writers have defined the subject of their studies: "the common man."

After noting the disappearance of the medieval idea of Everyman, de Certeau describes the slow development of a circumscribed category of "common men" whose characteristics were fixed by the time of the Enlightenment, and whose chief quality was that of being unlike the investigator. He analyzes a passage of Freud's *Civilization and Its Discontents*.

> Leaving aside the "small number" of "thinkers" and "artists" capable of transforming work into pleasure through sublimation, thus excluding that "rare elect" who nevertheless designate the place in which his text is elaborated, he signs a contract with "the ordinary man" and weds his discourse to the masses whose *common* destiny is to be duped, frustrated, forced to labor, and who are thus subject to the law of deceit and to the pain of death. . . . But is it not also true that Freudian theory derives an analogous advantage from the general experience it invokes? As the representative of an abstract universal, the ordinary man in Freudian theory still plays the role of a god who is recognizable in his effects, even if he has humbled himself and merged with the superstitious common people: he furnishes Freud's discourse with the means of *generalizing* a particular knowledge and of *guaranteeing* its validity by the whole of history. . . . He assures it of both its difference ("enlightened" discourse remains distinct from "common" discourse) and of its universality (enlightened discourse expresses and explains common experience). (Certeau 1984, 3)

Relating this passage to contemporary visual arts, in.s.omniac Thrilling Voice wrote of artist Barbara Kruger on IN.S.OMNIA, "The relationship between the artist/investigator and her subjects is forever: 'you have the problem, I have the insight' " (IN.S.OMNIA 1988).

In reply, Strange Justice entered the following anecdote.

> In a public conference in Paris in April 1987 reviewing the art of the preceding twenty years, whose participants included Umberto Eco, Paolo Fabbri, Alain Robbe-Grillet, Jean Baudrillard, Pierre Boulez, and others, the proposition was put forward by Eco, summarizing previous discussions, that one of the most common ideas in the artistic community of the '60s was the project of "making everyone an artist."
>
> The agreement of the conference participants seemed unanimous that this project had been "completely abandoned."
>
> We wonder if this idea has ever REALLY been tried. We wonder if it wasn't just a groovy thing to say. We wonder if Career Artists didn't dip their toes into this possibility and run screaming to safety when they realized what it might do to their privileged social position.
>
> Maurice Blanchot asked himself what would happen the moment the last writer on earth died. He replied that instead of silence one would hear a rising murmur—all those who had been silent for so long.
>
> Let's make IN.S.OMNIA the proving ground of these abandoned ideas. Let's tell the world that HERE ON IN.S.OMNIA WE CALL THE CRITICS' BLUFFS! (IN.S.OMNIA 1988)

These questions are not posed to suggest that there is or should be no such thing as a career writer. Just that there have been so many layers of worshipful varnish put over the definition of "writer" that it's now impossible to see what one might be.

In response to the explanation of creativity, "quality work comes from extraordinary people," and its corollary, the Situationists' "that which appears is good, that which is good appears," which is essentially mystical or metaphysical, some invisibles recognized in themselves a counterexplanation, no less metaphysical. This article of faith found its expression in this message blurted into the darkness of the bulletin board.

> ▌87jun02 from Foreperson
> Since IN.S.OMNIA is the place for unforgivable honesty, I will enter something I think a lot but have never dared to say. (Clears throat, stares at shoes.)
> Chester Anderson was right: "The proportion of Real People to Nerds is the same

**wherever you go." To this day I've never seen it disproved. At the biggest confer-
ence of the "brightest minds"—the proportion is always the same. Mostly nerds.
Worthwhile people . . . people who really, I mean really, "get it" are distributed
randomly and evenly around the globe, regardless of family, schooling, fame,
looks, poverty, etc. etc. etc. (IN.S.OMNIA)**▮

The Novel Project accessed this creativity through a hybrid of approaches.
There was the simple "describe your car" question and the "tell us your story,"
anthropological inquiry that underlay the entries in Proteus's Diary. But there also had been
other kinds of questions, such as the fill-in-the-blanks song and "Give us the name of a book
with the word Seattle in the title." The message of these other questions was "come play
with us."

This was the path that *Invisible America* needed to take. Asking people to tell
their stories is one thing. But *Invisible America* had to be designed to ask them to join in a
creative game, to fictionalize, tease, parody, mock, exaggerate—all the practices of everyday
creativity.

Anthropological inquiries generally demand that replies be honest, single-
leveled, responsible to a single voice. *Invisible America* would incite participants to invent a
voice or voices in which to respond. Everyday creativity, because it most often uses recycled
materials ironically recombined, takes place on at least two levels. It is always within *another*
context. Minimum: two levels at once.

But despite the clear ways in which IN.S.OMNIA makes use of everyday
creativity and the mega-project *Invisible America* promises further ways to tap its energy, a
troubling issue continues to rise. What are the power relationships such projects engender?
Are two people truly equal on a field of play when one of them has created the game? To
sketch an answer to this question, we must first attempt to understand the subtle dynamics
of creative collaboration.

exempli gratia viii

Sometimes the goals and the rules governing an activity are invented, or negotiated on the spot. For example, teenagers enjoy impromptu interactions in which they try to "gross each other out," or tell tall stories, or make fun of their teachers. The goal of such sessions emerges by trial and error, and is rarely made explicit; often it remains below the participants' level of awareness. Yet it is clear that these activities develop their own rules and that those who take part have a clear idea of what constitutes a successful "move," and of who is doing well. In many ways this is the pattern of a good jazz band, or any improvisational group. Scholars or debaters obtain similar satisfaction when the "moves" in their arguments mesh smoothly, and produce the desired result. (Csikszentmihalyi 1990, 56)

90jul05 from "Big Phone" Bill
I keep running across wonderful, creative people who produce fascinating magazines and posters and events but who insist, when I press them , "Oh, I'm not a writer," "I'm not an artist," "I JUST DO THIS STUFF." If our Chicago friend S . . . is not a writer, if our Boston friends S . . . and J . . . are not artists, then I no longer want to be a writer or an artist, I want to be WHATEVER IT IS that THEY are. (IN.S.OMNIA)

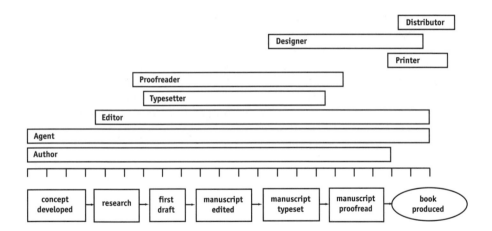

Pattern of collaboration in a text commonly supposed to be a "single author" text.

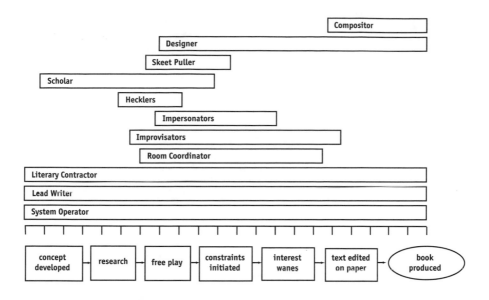

Pattern of collaboration in an IN.S.OMNIA project.

Only certain texts have authors, after all. Many others—such as computer programs or federal regulations—do not. (Ede and Lunsford 1990, 88)

We have even considered publishing major projects such as this book under coined neologisms, such as Annalisa Edesford or LisaAnn Lunede. (Ede and Lunsford 1990, xii)

We also asked Bernstein [psychologist Albert Bernstein] a question about the "pride of ownership" he felt when writing alone versus writing together. Again, his answer surprised us: "When I work with other people, one or two other people, I feel that I do a much better job than I would have done alone. I extend myself further and I think I have a clearer idea of what we are trying to do. *It brings more out of me so I think it is more mine.* I don't mind sharing the credit" (our emphasis). (Ede and Lunsford 1990, 29)

Acknowledging Collaboration: New Roles for Writers

Author, editor, publisher, reader—terms that no longer seem adequate. Troupe, user, Literary Worker—are these terms that credit what really occurs?

It was 1987—time to follow through on the initial joke of the Novel Project and extract from the overflowing data base a printed, bound, novel-like object. Starting with version 4.0 (the so-called Illustrated Manuscript version of 1984), this year saw more compilation at many hands and the slow accumulation of typeset pages, line art, and half-tones. But a troubling, practical question arose.

For the purposes of the massive data base of *Books in Print* (1948–), what should be the byline? Who should be credited as author? The invisibles' own credit history showed that *The Daily Zeitgeist* (Invisible Seattle 1983a) simply ran a paragraph of 8-point type with a grab-bag of names of participants, friends, and sponsors. The ordering was by descending degree of participation, judged subjectively as the deadline loomed.

The novel had to have a single byline if it was going to fit into American bookselling's tracking system. And it was of primary importance that the book be distributed and get into people's hands.

Latenight calls on the topic crossed the continent. What were the options? There was no way to include the names of all the participants. Inadequate records had been kept even of all the people who had gathered data in the white overalls and question-marked hard hats, let alone the thousands who lent a word, a phrase, a plot twist.

How had other literary collaborations managed the credit issue? There seemed to be several alternatives.

A work can be published with no names at all.

A work can be published, like the bestsellers of Victorian pornography, under the name "Anonymous." Names can be assigned by scholars, like "The Tristan Poet."

All of the contributors can be lumped under a single name, like, say, "Homer."

Names can be strung together with "ands" like Beaumont and Fletcher, Addison and Steele.

A single name from the group can occupy the byline, and subsidiary credit can be given within the book in various dedications, acknowledgments, postfaces, and colophons.

Certain contributions—those of the great American editors Maxwell Perkins and Saxe Commins, for example—are proudly recorded entirely outside the book in question—in memoirs, essays, and biographies. The purchaser of a volume of Fitzgerald, Wolfe, Hemingway, Faulkner, or O'Neill is never notified of the collaboration.

Also to be found outside the book—in even more obscure corners—are traces of collaborations more complex than professional editing. There is informal editing, like Ezra Pound's halving of *The Waste Land*. And what of collaborations by constant association, like the mutual reading aloud of Joseph Conrad and Ford Madox Ford? What of collaborations like the structural assistance rendered to James Joyce by Sylvia Beach?

After Sylvia's death, the Paris correspondent of the Guardian declared, "That Ulysses became the sort of book it is is largely due to her, for it was she . . . who decided to allow Joyce an indefinite right to correct his proofs. It was in the exercise of this right that the peculiarities of Joyce's prose style reached their novel flowering." (Fitch 1983, 106)

The fact that principal authorship remains uncontested in most of these cases still doesn't negate the collaboration. How much easier it would be if these cases were outright plagiarism or forgery (where the name of one author could simply be substituted for another) or clear alternations like Breton and Soupault's *Champs Magnétiques* where the handwritten manuscript allows the text to be attributed to one or the other author line by line.

No, as with everyday creativity, the questions raised at the end of the 20th century focus on the fraying borders of conventional practice as it is conventionally understood. It would be maddening for the conscientious scholar to have to take into account advice given in conversation and even the *oohs*, *aahs*, and *ughs* of the listener to whom a writer reads aloud. However, the creative practices of the future are taking shape at these borders.

Finally and distressingly, the research showed that credit for collaborations can simply be withheld, even suppressed. Contemporary scholarship (for example, Jack Stillinger's *Multiple Authorship and the Myth of Solitary Genius* [1991]) shows how Coleridge's borrowings have been consistently kicked under the carpet, how Mrs. Mill merits part credit for John Stuart's autobiography, how Mrs. Hawthorne participated in what's known as Nathaniel's work.

This concealing of credit indicated a sensitive complex of issues. What motivates the powerful tendency for credit to boil down to a single name?

The first answer to that question lies in a series of related concerns of accountability, marketing, and information management. Early in the history of bookselling the author's name was seized upon as a guarantee of a certain standard of quality by the book buyer and as a simple, shorthand marketing tool by the bookseller. In addition, publishers' and authors' names became a legal requirement in many realms, so that the crown could easily ascertain whom to punish. This legal/marketing shorthand continues to this day; *Books in Print* comes in only two flavors: Title and Author.

The second element of the answer was added with the historical rise of professional writers for whom piracy and mistaken credit meant missed income.

The third element enters most recently in the form of the "genius model," which, as we've noted, explains quality text as the product of the extraordinary individual.

But this three-part rationalization for boiling credit down to a single name is being severely taxed by contemporary collaborative writing practices—and *not* principally by the efforts of marginal literary experimentation. For example, working in collaboration is considered by many to be the chief distinguishing factor between modern science and premodern science. Lisa Ede and Andrea Lunsford in their book *Singular Texts/Plural Authors* ask:

> **Given the collaborative nature of modern science, why were those engaged in citation studies content to count only the first authors of multiauthored papers? Why did they not realize that ignoring all but the first author compromised their**

**efforts to determine the nature of scientific productivity and chart the structure
of modern science? (75)**

Ede and Lunsford's study points to collaboration as a norm, not an aberration, in the hard sciences, social sciences, and many areas of business. They observe a useful distinction between "hierarchical" and "dialogic" collaboration. Hierarchical collaboration in their definition has clear goals that are "most often designated by someone outside of and hierarchically superior to the immediate collaborative group or by a senior member or leader of the group. Because productivity and efficiency are of the essence in this mode of collaboration, the realities of multiple voices and shifting *authority* are seen as difficulties to be overcome or resolved" (133).

The rarer, "dialogic" collaboration on the other hand "is loosely structured and the roles enacted within it are fluid: one person may occupy multiple and shifting roles as a project progresses." "Furthermore," they propose, "those participating in dialogic collaboration generally value the creative tension inherent in multivoiced and multivalent ventures" (133).

Contemporary business theory, as well, is filled with postindustrial models of production based on teamwork and collaboration.

Viewed in this light, IN.S.OMNIA is clearly dialogic, and the Novel Project was unclearly a hybrid of both approaches used at different phases. But even in hierarchical phases, the invisible organizers' goal of becoming astonished permeated the proceedings.

The first two aspects of the credit dilemma—marketing and money—were of scarce theoretical concern for a group such as the invisibles. As with all marginal creatives, one tries for mainstream distribution or one doesn't; in either case, the chance of financial return is remote at best. The agreement among the invisibles was, as always, to plow back any profits into further projects.

The most intriguing compulsion toward a single name—the most needy of attention—was the genius system.

We understand that the genius system is a way of explaining where good work comes from—the quality book is a child of its quality author/parent. If the bloodline is assured, the quality is ensured.

Collaboration has been downplayed because it produces a mixed bloodline.

And what is more pedestrian, but even more problematic—real-life collaboration is complicated and hard to track. Part of the attraction of the genius system is its simplicity. Its explanation of the origin of good work has seemed as "natural" as the socioeconomic principle of male succession.

This broaches the general question of whether collaboration can produce good work. Considering the illustrious list of collaborations cited, the answer must be yes.

However, behind the simple formula of the genius system is a more addictive economy. The system works in two directions: It defines not only the book but the author also. The genius guarantees the book; the book proves the genius. To question the genius system is to question an important and widespread system of psychological self-definition. Resistance to reexamination of the system often boils down to a simple question: *If I'm not to be a genius, then what is my role in the world?*

A realistic examination of the roles available in the genius system shows that they are few and unequal. There is the *Genius* and its future and past forms: the *Wannabe* and the *Hasbeen*. All that's left is the *Courtier*, that necessary concomitant, that Enabler, that Co-dependent who allows it all to happen by being the editor, the publisher, the reviewer, the biographer, the long-suffering spouse or lover. As in.s.omniac Ruebrick puts it,

Isn't a genius like a Japanese Bunraku puppet? Behind the brightly illuminated, lifelike, wonderful figure is a team of puppeteers, dressed in black, hooded in black, who make it all happen. The human being who shares name and face with the puppet genius may indeed be the chief puppeteer, the one who controls the figure's head, the right hand. But the others are necessary for the whole trick to work. (IN.S.OMNIA 1990)

Sadly, the genius system is often charged with fear, haunted by the notion that there is only a fixed, small amount of room in the spotlight at any one time. Those in the dark are desperately jealous of those who occupy the light and are miserable even once they reach the glare, afraid of the younger ones to follow. This is the haunted, aristocratic sleep of the sovereign who reigns, terrified, in the sacred grove, waiting for the successor whose first act must be assassination.

For in.s.omniacs, relief from this gloomy prospect lies in having discovered a multitude of other roles a writer can slip into depending on the moment's chemistry of passion, personality, and available time.

For what use it may be, here is a quick accounting of the roles observed in Invisible Seattle projects and on IN.S.OMNIA.

One key find was the list of St. Bonaventure included in J. A. Burrow's *Medieval Writers and Their Work* and cited in Ian Haywood's *Faking It: Art and the Politics of Forgery.*

> **Sometimes a man writes other's words, adding nothing and changing nothing; and he is simply called a scribe [*scriptor*]. Sometimes a man writes other's words, putting together passages which are not his own; and he is called a compiler [*compilator*]. Sometimes a man writes both other's words and his own, but with the other's words in prime place and his own added only for purposes of clarification [*commentator*]. Sometimes a man writes both his own words and other's, but with his own in prime place, and other's added only for purposes of clarification; and he should be called an author [*auctor*]. (Haywood 1987, 16)**

Another key ingredient was formulated in *The Plan for Invisible America.* It extended a term used during the Novel Project: "Literary Contractors." As the *Plan* details:

> **The only activities that differentiate Career Writers from other Artists with Words are: (1) making a record of their verbal creativity, (2) doing the drudge work of patching and smoothing it into big pieces, and (3) attempting to make those larger pieces public. It is precisely these activities that, as Literary Contractors, we propose to take care of in *Invisible America*. Everyday creativity of occasional writers plus competent literary contracting equals an electronic game/novel worth the price of admission. (*IN.S.OMNIA Print Outs 1* 1987)**

Around St. Bonaventure's list of roles the following could be assembled.

Literary Contractor, one who works to provide the physical infrastructure, conceptual algorithm, and energetic enthusiasm that it takes to realize a full project. This role subsumes many of the functions of editor and publisher. It best reflects the impulse voiced by an in.s.omniac who wrote that she wanted to paraphrase the cry of the ambitious Hollywood denizen: "I no longer want merely to *write*, I want to *produce*."

System Operator, a term taken straight from the computer world (along with its short form, *Sysop*), designates the hard-working person who not only keeps the system up and running technically but also performs those aspects of the traditional editor's role that include weeding out the gibberish, hand-holding the technologically timid, and acting as on-line ombudsman for users whose egos get tender or fall into squabbles with other users.

Room Coordinator is a role assumed by someone who serves many of the purposes of a Literary Contractor but whose project is contained within the single medium of the bulletin board.

Lead Writer is the term for someone who takes a special interest in a certain project or room and makes it the focus of a brilliant and formative series of messages. The Lead Writer's role is often, but not necessarily, shared with the Literary Contractor or Room Coordinator's roles. A Room Coordinator may start but lose interest in a room, only to have it vitalized by a self-appointed Lead Writer who seizes the idea and takes it in an unexpected direction.

Improvisator is the latinate term for a role modeled on improvisational comedy. A real-time partner in crime, the Improvisator contributes to a project or room by subscribing to the improv dictum of always saying "yes, and," rather than "no, but" to another user's contribution.

Impersonator, or pure stylist. This term describes the breathtaking mastery of voices and writing styles that is some users' specialty. These are the "go to" users that one *goes to* for help when a project or room is in need of a particularly spectacular passage. "We need one of your brooding soliloquies here." "How about one of those cascading lists now?"

Heckler, the scoffer, the reality check, the user who chimes into an overearnest exchange with a healthy "aw, get over yourself!"

Scholar is the term for the specialists of linkage. These users scour history and the present for useful messages, project structures, and critical analogies, entering apt citations as contribution and counterpoint to the work in progress.

Skeet Puller is the term coined to identify the user who is always able to throw out ideas—good, bad, appropriate, inappropriate—like a never-ending fountain of clay pigeons, skeet-shooting targets. Invaluable for getting a stalled project out of the doldrums.

Listener—based on the image of the author reading aloud to a trusted friend— the user who perfects a composition in progress simply by perceiving it, by being known to be a user on the system. The one whose high standards make everyone else strive harder.

Designer, the specialist in the visual and verbal synergies of the printed page.

Compositor, as in typesetter. Every publishing professional knows how many gaffes are spared the public by the eagle-eyed queries of a good typesetter.

This preliminary list—far from precise, far from complete—is given as an indication of the typologies that may help reshape creative users' self-definitions.

Among in.s.omniacs, the role of Literary Contractor tends to be taken on by those who, in their visible lives, consider or considered themselves to be "authors." But *The Plan for Invisible America*'s distinction between "Career Writers" and "Other Artists with Words" raises an interesting distinction.

Doesn't it really boil down to a self-defined difference between people who consider writing "the main thing" that they do and those who consider writing "a thing" that they do? We could call them "full-time" writers and "occasional" writers. The existing genius system dismisses occasional writers a priori, the sense being that a kind of vow of life vocation, on the model of a religious order, is a requirement for serious consideration. Work on IN.S.OMNIA has shown no need to discriminate between full-time and occasional participants. One of the most intriguing aspects of the bulletin board is the way in which Literary Contractors and Room Coordinators help occasional writers make the best use of their writing time.

Once authorship as a vocation has been demystified, doesn't it become apparent that all writers go through periods when they cannot write, for a variety of economic and practical reasons? So the descriptors "full-time writer" and "occasional writer" may apply best not to discrete individuals but to periods in the lives of those individuals. Any number of people, people who would never describe themselves as authors, may be passionate "full-time writers" for a while. The same people, and many more, may spend wonderful, odd moments of their lives as "occasional writers." Writing becomes projects and their moments, not people and their vocations.

It gets even more complicated as one person may take on more than one role at a time during the different phases of a project, and these combinations of roles may change from phase to phase.

On IN.S.OMNIA, one user may be the Room Coordinator of one room and participate in others as an Impersonator and Skeet Puller.

In the course of a project, one person may begin as a Literary Contractor in the research and planning phase. Then, during the data-gathering phase, the demands of a money-earning occupation may change that person's role to that of an occasional Improvisator and Heckler. Later, that person may contribute the skills of Scriptor and Compositor to the project's publication phase. By the standards of the genius system, this typical example of creative involvement is a failure. On IN.S.OMNIA, this participation is appreciated and credited.

What emerges is a paradigm of writing as a behavior, something anyone can perform from time to time—a job, a task, a passion, a hobby—rather than a calling, a vocation, an election, or an inheritance. Beside the cataclysmic birthing cycle of inspiration, creation, production, and despondency exists the in.s.omniac's steady habit of calling the bulletin board (late, when the phone rates are cheap) to play and advance several concurrent projects. Although this model may not be as spectacular as the romanticized one, it is just as pleasurable. It also has the advantage of meshing with the rest of reality.

The list given here is not a complete solution to the troubling power inequalities of the "enlightener vs. common man" model discussed in the preceding chapter. It redistributes power, but there is still the phenomenon of leadership. Authority to make final edits of print publications still generally rests in the hands of the Literary Contractors—according to the dictum "I brought the bat and ball, I get to declare the game over." The roles developed not from a direct search for equality of power, but from a search for projects that are fresh and interesting—an aesthetic search. Continued theoretical work must be done to understand and trace and disentangle those strands of power.

When the time comes to credit such projects, what recourse is there? Perhaps the answer lies in the direction of the heady, rambling lists of friends' names that crowd pop music CD packaging and often find their way into the lyrics of rap songs themselves.

Perhaps the model of film credits can be adapted, even though it generally pins a single name into a single role. We imagine a book with film-type credits: the publisher's name alone appears on the cover. Several pages of text follow. A Lead Writer's name appears. More text. Another name, then another. More text. Finally the title is revealed. The main portion of the text follows, and the remaining contributors' names are jammed together at the end.

The 6" x 9" version of the Novel Project, it was finally and uneasily decided, should contain no names. Its byline would be the same as its title: *Invisible Seattle*.

An uneasy solution because undue credit might be conferred on those publicly associated with the group.

The issue of credit for the Novel Project turned on the assumption that participants desired, and were owed, accurate credit. But the pseudonymity and anonymity rampant on IN.S.OMNIA provokes a deeper doubt. There is a persistent and rebellious refusal to take credit, a desire to remain truly anonymous, a profound questioning of *who may take credit* for even the solitary product of a single person.

----

exempli gratia ix

▌85feb14 from Mehitabel
Where am I? Who am I? I was lost in the electron storm, and I'm just
unscrambling myself now.▌

▌85feb14 from Tom McBride
the person you see on the boards is real, the one you might meet on the
street is a 'nym.▌

▌85feb14 from tyrone slothrop
i'm not sure i like the idea of me, tyrone, describing that "rob" person
. . . it hurts that sludge that i call "my brain" . . .
i am schitzo enuf without your encouragement, ken▌

▌85feb14 from marquis d'maypo
well, i do know for a positive fact that mehitabel once said of me that i
was only person that she had met face from the boards who looked just
like he typed▌

▌85feb145 from T'an T'u
My human is fairly bright, of slightly more than "average" height, and
a discerning eye. he misses little of what he sees and often reads phi-
losophy & sociology text to help him rationalize people's actions. . . .

▌85feb15 from liz mahoney
Since I asked the question I guess I should step up and answer for my
'nym. I am somebody dead! The name belongs to my deceased
Grandmother . . . (IN.S.OMNIA)▌

"I'm black, male, at the bottom of the social heap," he says. "I'm castrated in drag. But I'm also freed. There's a sort of cultural Judgment Day going on. Everybody's been forced to come out of the closet, in all kinds of ways, not just sexually. And when they get out I'm here to tell them, "Smile, laugh, welcome to the party!" (RuPaul, Supermodel, in Trebay 1993)

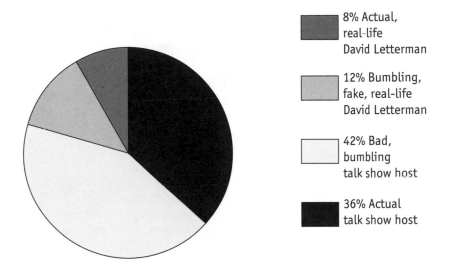

8% Actual, real-life David Letterman

12% Bumbling, fake, real-life David Letterman

42% Bad, bumbling talk show host

36% Actual talk show host

Self as a function of ironically contradictory levels of sincerity in a show-business persona. Case study: television talk-show host David Letterman as he appeared in 1989.

Once the explanatory narratives have been digested, the newly illuminated reader may hurtle uncontrollably *but safely* into the more profound, esoteric and, mayhaps, *frightening* tales—those designed to disconnect established thought patterns and sabotage habitual mental logic. . . . This arrangement allows the reader to become gradually familiar not only with the ancillary characters who populate the later stories, *but even with their writing styles*—for did not these so-called "characters" *write* half the stories? (Dr. Philo Drummond, OverMan 1st Degree, First Authorized FisTemple Lodge, Church of the SubGenius/Drummondian—found in Stang 1990, 17)

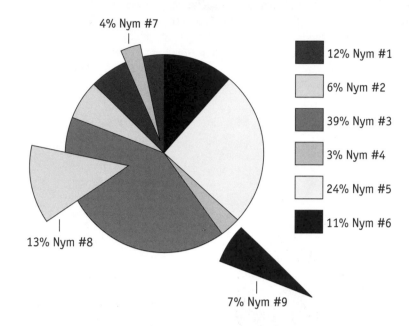

4% Nym #7

12% Nym #1

6% Nym #2

39% Nym #3

3% Nym #4

24% Nym #5

11% Nym #6

13% Nym #8

7% Nym #9

Self as a function of mutually contradictory 'nyms employed by a single user of IN.S.OMNIA. Case Study: User X, 1985–86. Note that one of the chief results of the division of self into 'nyms is, as User X put it, "Fragments of personality that you don't normally acknowledge appear on the board. You put the pieces of your self together and they add up to more than one hundred percent."

84sep22 from Eugene Correct
Using words to replicate, with symbols, your own ego on this board is a fairly tiresome and probably futile task to undertake. You'll never suc-ceed. In fact, the less you try, the more you will succeed. Words are personalities in and of themselves. So pick your words like you pick your friends—engage the ones you like, avoid the ones you don't like. Allow us sometimes the opportunity to get to know you by the company you keep, the words you choose to associate with. They aren't just your words, we all share them, as we may share friends. We are here to PLAY. (IN.S.OMNIA)

❚93mar25 from MEI LAN GUZMAN-CHANG
My great-uncle Irving Berlin told me that William Makepeace Thackeray
told him that he and Zachary Taylor had once been lovers. Thackeray
was a high-school senior at the time, and Zachary Taylor a hack Ohio
politician and the most notorious "chicken hawk" in the Columbus-
Dayton-Akron tri-cities area. This was at a time when my revered ancestor owned a restaurant in Columbus, called the Pho An Quahn Tacqueria
Spot. Uncle Irving and I had a good laugh over the name of revered
ancestor's restaurant, because in English "Pho An Quahn" would mean
"Very Lucky Citadel of Good Digestion," while at the same time, in
Yiddish, it means (with a very slight homophonic distortion) something
very close to "Fuck the Police." Revered ancestor's friends and family
(so Thackeray told Berlin) had often urged him, having been convinced
by his astrologer that this was a marvelously felicitous name for a retail
food establishment, and, moreover, that it was his extraordinary good
luck that no other restaurant operator in Eastern Ohio had already
taken it.❚

❚93apr08 from Interior Boy
My GOD!!!! These messages from this purported Guzman-Chang person
are the MOST OFFENSIVE pure SHIT that I've encountered since last
week, when I had the misfortune to read Jeff Koons's commentary on
his own oeuvre-to-date. I mean, this stuff is anti-Semitic, homophobic
and Asian-bashing, plus it's full of ludicrious historical and geographical errors. Columbus is NOT in eastern Ohio, for starters. And Bill
Thackeray DID NOT write novels with ridiculous names like *Siberian
Jews Living in Beverly Hills*. He was an English novelist, never American,
could not possibly have met Zachary Taylor, and he wrote novels with
serious names like *Vanity Fair* (which he swiped out of Bunyan's
Pilgrim's Progress). And politicians that have sex with high school
seniors are not called "chicken hawks" any more; they're called "child
molesters." And so on and so forth, my point being that I've always
HATED this bulletin board because they'll let TOTALLY TWISTED WEIRDO
LIARS say any gosh-darned thing that pops into their crazy minds and
everyone acts like it's normal or something. (IN.S.OMNIA)❚

chapter 9

Doing Voices: Since Each of Us Was Several

How we envy an IN.S.OMNIA user in the first few weeks of usership. In a matter of days new users get to experience firsthand what theoreticians debate at length—a concept of the mind based on the analogy of the book versus a mind modeled on the fluid world of messages. Not that the pleasures don't get richer over time, but nothing quite matches that honeymoon when one exhausts oneself with the joy of 'nyms.

You, the beginner, are plunged into a system that uses messages tagged with user names, known as " 'nyms." You respond to a message or a flow of messages with the greatest contrast you can conceive. Or—even more surprising—you decide to follow a message with a continuation that mimics precisely the style of its precedent. You ransack your mind and your library for inappropriate styles, entering wild parodies and pastiches that enlarge the room with ironic tangles of form and content.

The scribbled list of your alter ego 'nyms and their passwords grows beside you keyboard. A new 'nym is often just the touch needed to send a room into the proper tailspin.

85feb08 from Desperado # One
Alright, nobody move!!

85feb08 from SOUND EFFECTS
(a crowd gasping, hub-bub, screams) . . .

85feb08 from Desperado # One
This is a hijacking! We're hijacking IN.S.OMNIA. Everyone in the Derrida room is a hostage . . .

▌8 5 f e b 0 8   f r o m   S O U N D   E F F E C T S
(click)▌

▌8 5 f e b 0 8   f r o m   R h e t t   B u t l e r
Frankly my dear, I don't give▌

▌8 5 f e b 0 8   f r o m   S O U N D   E F F E C T S
(click)▌

▌8 5 f e b 0 8   f r o m   K e n n y   R o g e r s
four hungry children and crop in the▌

▌8 5 f e b 0 8   f r o m   S O U N D   E F F E C T S
(click)▌

▌8 5 f e b 0 8   f r o m   D a n   R a t h e r
are holding a room in Invisible Seattle's IN.S.OMNIA BBS hostage, in an apparent
attempt to hijack the board. They have yet to give any reason for their actions.▌

▌8 5 f e b 0 8   f r o m   H a p l e s s   U s e r
Oh please, please, won't you let my husband log out? He has a heart condition,
I'm very worried for him, have MERCY!! (IN.S.OMNIA)▌

Then there comes a moment when, in reply to some delicious bon mot entered under a new 'nym, another user addresses you by one of your old 'nyms! Aaagh! You've been found out. Your style has given you away. What a disappointment. The skills you've honed, the styles you've developed seem careworn and few. You want to crawl out of your own skin.

So you begin to study the style of the others' 'nyms more closely. You try them out on scratch pads, like rehearsing in the shower. Tentatively you test the new styles on the board itself, realizing that they give you access to trains of thought you never would have taken before. Soon your bag of tricks, your stylistic costume chest, is growing. You have more and more ways to think and react.

Although this is a learning process, it is also an unlearning.

▌9 1 j a n 0 2   f r o m   P e r s o n
Writing on the board makes the way i used to write, the way i was taught to
write, seem like taking the menagerie of voices in my head and stuffing them

into a big pastry bag so they can be squzz out of the funnel in a nice, bland line. On IN.S.OMNIA i just give those little voices names and let them squeak for themselves. They say things i THINK ALL THE TIME but would never sign my own name to. If other voices disagree with them i sign on as them AND LET THEM ANSWER BACK.▌

▌9 1 j a n 0 4 f r o m N E T H E R L A N S
. . . It's like you usually have this internal debate about what to write, and the "debaters" whoever they are hammer out a compromise. Here we write the debate, not the compromise. (IN.S.OMNIA)▌

This urge to further and further differentiation not just among one's characters but one's "authors" surpasses the heteroglossia of a single novel with a single author's name on the cover.

The search for companions in this mode of working reveals an alternate tradition. There is the great beacon, Perec, who wanted to make each of his books as different as possible from the others and who expressed the desire to write one of everything, every genre.

There are the literary hoaxters such as French novelist Romain Gary, who won the Goncourt Prize under his own name, then brought out in the 1970s a series of novels published under the name Emile Ajar. Concealing the identity of Ajar even from his publishers, Gary persuaded a young relative to play the part, having him refuse "Ajar's" Goncourt Prize.

But IN.S.OMNIA's chief historical friend must be the Portuguese poet Fernando Pessoa, who employed the term "heteronym" for the names under which he published. Among the most important of his heteronyms were Ricardo Reis, the anarchist doctor (born in 1887, a year before Pessoa himself), Alberto Caeiro the naive poet of nature, and the robust Alvaro de Campos with his superb, almost classical tone.

The paths of these companions bring into relief a set of assumptions about the relationship of authors and styles, often referred to as the author's "voice." The common assumption is that one unique author, one self, possesses one unique voice and that the goal of a self's creative life is first to find its voice, and then to use it exclusively, forsaking all others.

This outlook on the creative life often constitutes the subject matter of texts, where fictional characters and a host of narrating "*I*'s" seek self-knowledge and self-refinement in the course of experiencing a sequence of events. The reader participates not only in the texts' representations of narrators' and characters' finding themselves but also in the author's similar refinement of a self and its voice.

These two interrelated systems are what is meant when some in.s.omniacs somewhat cavalierly refer to "self-centered" writing. Self-centered writing takes a certain amount of good-natured bashing on the bulletin board.

▌89dec04 from Person
What a sordid display is the short story writer's precious fiction on one hand and earnest, coy interview on the other. They're two sides of the same worn coin— equally fictional. (IN.S.OMNIA)▌

But setting aside this kind of intemperate venting, it remains that the mad dash on IN.S.OMNIA to imitate other styles renders moot the search for a "natural" or "authentic" voice—the voice a particular person simultaneously *has a right* and *is condemned* to use. "Here," as one user put it, "everyone's voice is equally inauthentic" (IN.S.OMNIA).

What other goals might there be for texts and the creative life, goals that correspond to the modes of IN.S.OMNIA? As always the answer lies not in a simple revolution where one totalizing system is replaced by its totalizing opposite. The answer lies in pieces around us, in activities that have never ceased but have been left in the shadows while others are spotlighted.

One crucial thread is the tradition of carnival and those remnants of carnival tradition such as Halloween and Mardi Gras. Carnival can be viewed as a vacation for the single self, the letting off of steam that brings a not-entirely-stable system of self back to equilibrium. Carnival is evidence of the year-round repression of multiple selves.

Another fruitful model is the tradition of comic impersonators. They, too, try to add voices to their collection. They must go from voice to voice as celebrities come and go.

Especially interesting are Jonathan Winters and his student Robin Williams who break down the skit format and shift quickly from character to character. They hold dialogues with themselves and play off of input from the audience. These entertainers make comedy out of the open destruction of the "one actor to one character" formula. What a contrast between, say, a Robert DeNiro who is clearly Robert DeNiro the actor outside of a film, and consistently Jake LaMotta within the film. Robin Williams on stage is neither clearly any one of his characters nor clearly Robin Williams. He is several characters and several Robin Williamses at once. Minimum: two selves.

When this multi-leveled comedy is schematized, it is remarkably similar to everyday creativity: given roles in given situations, played out with subversive irony and bristling with levels of voiced impersonation.

But what about pushing beyond the point of one "real person," one self who "does" several voices?

This seemingly dangerous line of inquiry—the fragmentation of the self—is actually quite familiar. We commonly talk of being different people at home from what we are at work or with our parents.

During the period of the Surrealist *sommeils*, those frightening parlor experiments with self-hypnosis and automatic writing, Robert Desnos slumps into a bizarre state and writes uncontrollably. The texts are published under Desnos's name, but who is writing? While still walking through the role of the genius, the Surrealists in practice, like the in.s.omniacs, were more interested in the text and its powers than the author and hers or his.

A more explicit admission of the situation comes from Gilles Deleuze and Félix Guattari who begin their collaborative *A Thousand Plateaus* with these words, "The two of us wrote *Anti-Oedipus* together. Since each of us was several, there was already quite a crowd" (1987, 3).

Psychology from Freud to *I'm OK, You're OK* is full of labels for various internal voices. It is only taking half a step to give them individual 'nyms, Igor instead of ego, Ida instead of id.

Then there are the courageous (for all their exuberant nonchalance) spectacles of the postmodern drag queen movement, which reaches its most public flowering in events such as New York's Wigstock. Lady Bunny, RuPaul, Fertile Latoyah Jackson, Vaginal Creme Davis, and the others simply *are* different people at different times and don't really worry about it. They have nothing to gain by sticking to a single self, as their "selves" reckoned by the traditional structure are already threatened with violent exclusion by society.

"We don't want to make the old mistake of romanticizing mental illness," writes IN.S.OMNIA's Person. "Some kind of 'control,' in layman's terms, of a life is plainly a good thing. I'm just wondering —psychologist users chime in please—if control might NOT be identical with a single self but more of a baton that is passed from self to self" (IN.S.OMNIA 1989).

These examples demonstrate the complexity of the situation: within a single body, multiple selves "do" multiple voices. "Franny is listening to a program on wolves. I say to her, Would you like to be a wolf? She answers haughtily, How stupid, you can't be one wolf, you're always eight or nine, six or seven" (Deleuze and Guattari 1987, 29). ⸱

In.s.omniacs are pack animals, and for all the usefulness of the comparisons so far, we haven't broached the further complication of collaboration.

Obviously, a *group* of comic impersonators is an even better analogy for IN.S.OMNIA than an individual comic. A group of comic impersonators who share a pool of voices that each can do with greater or lesser effect. The specialists are called upon when needed to do their best voice.

Instead of the one-human-being-to-one-self-to-one-voice equation, a typical IN.S.OMNIA project might be charted as including seven human beings, twelve selves, and fifteen voices. Tracking the combinations is a daunting critical task.

The old Art vs. Life opposition depends as much on the stability of a notion of life as it does on the notoriously slippery definition of art. What if the self and the voice, or the selves and voices are rotisserie leagues of each other? What if they are interpenetrating and continuous, not an object and its reflection?

How does one react to a text such as this? Besides participating in it that is, as this infectious form not only makes you want to participate but also demands it. What's in it for the user? What are the pleasures of such a play of masks in such a non-place? The exquisite, context-dependent, efficient pleasures of multi-level communication. To write something as yourself can be satisfying communication. But to write something *as someone else* (another specific person or another type of person) triggers an instant contextual richness that would take hundreds of laborious words to explain.

Added to this "quick reference" quality are the multiple ironies of the contrast between who one "is" (for the moment) and whom one is claiming to be. These ironies also are much more easily "done" than explained. The fluidity of the "quick changes" possible increases this richness. Rather than struggling to supply your own context and then work within it, contexts on IN.S.OMNIA are being supplied constantly by other users, as you supply theirs. This inundation by contradictory contexts is a fragment of the day-to-day culture that surrounds the board and its users.

Timing in a theatrical sense is crucial to the artistry of a bulletin board. This is sadly apparent when reading the printed archives. They are sometimes like the side-splitting incident that falls flat in the retelling. IN.S.OMNIA shares with everyday creativity the apologia "I guess you had to be there."

Representative art seeks to change its readers by simulation. IN.S.OMNIA seeks to change by participation. The aesthetic desire lurking on IN.S.OMNIA to have it be forever unclear how many and which specific human beings are involved means that issues of credit may become as unimportant as at a party. The single-name system operates economically by traceable, single-unit sales, but the pressure may be off the single brand name if costs are covered by a price for admission.

The aesthetics likely to be emphasized in the coming period are those of impersonation, webs of irony, and formal sabotage.

85feb08 from Desperado # 3
1, tie THEM up!

85feb08 from Desperado # One
I'm not gonna do it unless you say I can hold the rocket launcher later, OK?

85feb08 from Desperado # 3
Yeah, OK.

85feb08 from Dan Rather
tying the hostages up. The hijackers appear calm but are arguing about who gets to hold the bazooka.

85feb08 from Bystander # One
Can't he tell it's a rocket launcher? They just SAID it's a rocket launcher.

85feb08 from Bystander # 2
I think those news guys deliberately get things wrong sometimes, just to throw their weight around. Now everybody in the world, and for the rest of time, will think that these hijackers had a bazooka, just because it was reported that way. . . . (IN.S.OMNIA)

This brings us to the idea—terror in some cases—that there is a dangerous, linking, hypertext model of mind beginning to usurp the revered book model of mind. This notion is sometimes used to discourage projects such as IN.S.OMNIA. We are pleased to report that there is nothing to fear.

First, claims for a book-based mind in past societies where only a tiny percentage of people were literate and had access to books are questionable.

Second, one must set aside claims made about the writing culture of past societies based on surviving texts without adjustments for the fact that many important, perhaps central, texts have vanished, and little basic information about size of libraries, reading habits, and so on, is known. Recent feminist history alone is enough to convince us of how much more we don't know than we used to. Short of a freakish archeological godsend, nothing substantial will ever be known about the various transitions from oral cultures to written cultures. Any story of the movement from speaking to writing is just that: a story, and cannot form the basis of a scientific analogy to the present time.

The linking mind, to play with the idea for a moment, would not conquer and occupy the same exact space in the psychocultural landscape as the book mind. The linking mind would incorporate large parts of the book mind and form a new constellation, including new areas. The new areas would include "nonliterary" academic disciplines such as communications and graphic design, alongside many forms of pop culture.

Fluidity, efficiency of multiple reference, impersonation—these are the survival skills of the information age.

exempli gratia x

▌9 3 j u n 1 7   f r o m   b a c k g r o u n d   n o i s e
People have stopped asking where you're from. They ask what you're connected to. (IN.S.OMNIA)▌

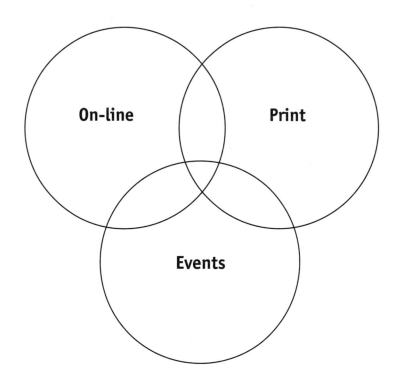

The interlocking zones in which IN.S.OMNIA projects take shape.

A Project Takes Shape
Fragments from the Drafting of Constitutions Unlimited 1987–89

87oct09 from Person
(Here's some copy for the handbill to promote the big event.)

Delegate Yourself!
Design your own constitution with
THE CUSTOM CONSTITUTION QUESTIONNAIRE
It's easy! It's Fun! It's binding!

1) I want my constitution to claim to derive its authority from:
  - a) The People
  - b) God
  - c) Male Landowners
  - d) Myself and a few friends in the military
  - e) Any suitable capitalized noun

2) My constitution will take effect when it is:
  - a) Conceived
  - b) Written
  - c) Signed
  - d) Published
  - e) Ratified
  - f) Backed by military force

3) My constitution will cease to be in effect when:
   a) It no longer reflects a consensus of rational beings
   b) The last written copy is destroyed
   c) A new one has taken its place
   d) It is no longer enforceable
   e) My constitution is eternal

4) My constitution will have its primary existence in:
   a) Its written form
   b) The minds of those who read it
   c) The hearts of the people
   d) The flesh of its victims
   e) The ensemble of actions it dictates and constrains

5) I want my constitution to place power in the hands of:
   a) The One
   b) The Few
   c) The Many
   d) My relatives
   e) The outfield of the Seattle Mariners

6) My constitution should be written so as to be understood only by:
   a) Legal professionals
   b) The college educated
   c) The overwhelmingly ambitious
   d) Amiable illiterates
   e) Anyone familiar with the visible works of Pierre Menard

Constitutions Unlimited
The Northwest's first full-service constitution store

87oct09 from Multatuli

Folks, it's party time again on IN.S.OMNIA. Our November writing jam approaches and you are all invited to participate, on the board or in person. November is the month when emissaries from the French group Oulipo arrive in Seattle to join us in launching a text. American poet and novelist Harry Mathews and French poet and novelist Jacques Roubaud will be here. Our first event takes place November 10 at 7:30 at Elliot Bay Books. That's a Tuesday. You are invited to come down and bring a constitution of your choice (other than the U.S.)—the Confederate perhaps, the French, any of the twenty-three Bolivian ones. We plan to transform them by Oulipean procedures (check the Oulipo room for more info) and use them as the basis of the following fiction.

CONSTITUTIONS UNLIMITED is the name of a boutique in fashionable Rainier Square, I believe, located between an espresso bar and a jewelry store. Perhaps you're looking for something bicameral and perpetually binding, or maybe something dictated, written or forged by God, perhaps your high school football team is in need of some compact to bond them during a losing season or you and your friends are contemplating a secessionist Republic or a rural nunnery—whatever your situation, Pierre Roussel and François Perec, the amiable French entrepreneurs who founded the boutique, will be happy to oblige you with a constitution to order for a nominal fee. Hence the name of this singular enterprise, chosen after carefully weighing the alternatives like CONSTITUTIONS R US or THE CONSTITUTION CONNECTION.

87oct11 from "Big Phone" Bill

The (Nosy) Apartment Neighbor's Constitution
—Preamble—
SEEING AS HOW I've been in this apartment house now longer than anyone else (excepting for Mr. A—on the third floor, who doesn't count), and how this building was the site of my happiest days including the joys, rages & indolence of my late Husband, and how therefore with more emotion & remembers invested in this place than anyone else it belongs more to me, and furthermore how at my advanced years I have less emotional good to expect from the rest of life, it incumbs upon me to have the biggest say in what goes on around here including the doings of other residents in the hallways, the front sidewalk, the laundry room, the dumpster, the dumpster area, the parking spaces, the alley immediately behind the building to a distance of 25 yards either way, and extending to right inside their apartments insofar as evidence of these doings is lookable or listenable.

8 8 j a n 0 6 f r o m C l a r k H u m p h r e y

When Constitutions Unlimited invented the personal constitution we were alone in the field. Now, in today's increasingly competitive legislation market, we stay on top by keeping up with all the newest trends (those few that we didn't start ourselves).

Many locations report great success with the new "impulse item" line of inexpensive, pre-packaged mini-constitutions sold at counter displays in blister pacs. The Safe Sex Constitution, packaged with a quality prophylactic, has generated news-media interest in Portland, Phoenix, Juneau, WITHOUT unduly exploiting public fears. We are, after all, in the business of personal security. Media calls should be forwarded to the national Public Information Office, E-mail Stop 1206.

8 8 j a n 1 5 f r o m i n v e n t e d g o d

COVER LETTER FOR FRANCHISE KIT
YOU
YOUR ADDRESS
YOUR CITY

We certainly appreciate your interest in becoming a Constitutions Unlimited franchisee. We think we have a great business opportunity. Already, numerous stores are open across the country and in Canada, however, we are a young company and have territories available practically anywhere you may wish to pursue.
The package you will find enclosed should assist you in your early review. Contact us at any time and I hope we can soon welcome you into the Constitutions Unlimited family.
Sincerely,
François and Pierre

8 8 j a n 2 0 f r o m M u l t a t u l i

Excellent genre! A kit for the prospective franchisee. The reader now has an identity. Our goal: to persuade our reader to leave his or her armchair and open up a Constitution Unlimited franchise. The reader is probably someone who could use the bucks, right? "Opening this book was your lucky day. A new and exciting future awaits you in the private legislation field . . ." And so on. The given form: the newspaper articles, ad slicks, sample letters, etc. of the business kit. Relentlessly optimistic.

88sep09 from The Vice Editor
From: Table of Contents, Franchisee's Confidential Operations Manual
Section III About Constitutions Unlimited, "The Company You Keep"
A. Official chronology of CU
B. Small business magazine article
C. Organizational chart
D. Job descriptions
E. In-house newsletter
  1. Diary of a Shopkeeper, by François
  2. Speech, by Pierre
  3. Goofy, embarrassing staff incentive program
  4. News from the company retreat (photos, accounts, reproductions of chalk-talk drawings)
  5. Hints of the secret superprogram

88sep11 from Person
What will our Constitutions Store look like? You are free to imagine just about anything, but the vision I get is of one of those shopping-center law-office franchises, decorated in the manner of one of the more precious Columbia Center law firms: Roman columns made of aluminum in the lobby, scattered and supporting nothing; a relief-mural Mercator projection of the world along one wall; suitable art works from the proper Pioneer Square galleries along the other wall; a high ceiling with recessed lighting fixtures (no glaring fluorescent bulbs in sight); dark-green carpeting; a newly-made but old-style wooden, waist-high partition between the lobby and the work area, traversed through a matching gate. In the open work area, clients and Constitutional Consultants meet at large oak desks. A wide variety of constitutions and contracts are available for customizing on the computer work stations. From there, they can be printed in several formats: official legal documents, parchment scrolls, Post-It Notes.

88sep20 from The Vice Editor
From: Table of Contents, Franchisee's Confidential Operations Manual
Section IV Crisis! What Brings Customers Into Your Store?
A. Legal Sales Imagination: Putting Yourself in the Customer's Shorts
B. Konstitution Kraze articles (*Time, Newsweek,* newspapers)
C. Catalog: describing the full CU product line
D. Advertising: Making it Work For You!

88oct12 from Clark Humphrey
SAMPLE ADS
From *Cosmopolitan* ad, showing a young woman with flaming blonde hair and bare shoulders:
"I know what I want in a man. And now, my men know it too. Because I've put it in writing. It's all in my Pocket Constitution, from Constitutions Unlimited. It's a tiny plastic card. Convenient enough to carry in the smallest purse or pocket. I hand it out with my phone number."
From *Rolling Stone/Spin* ad, showing a phony newspaper clipping of want ads selling used musical instruments above the following copy:
THEY THOUGHT THEY DIDN'T NEED A BAND CONSTITUTION.
They figured they could just "rock out together" and it'd all be OK. Those scathing break-ups that happened to other bands at the brink of success? "It just couldn't happen to us."
But it did.
Because they didn't have a Musical Constitution from Constitutions Unlimited.

88nov02 from Person

We recommend the following procedure to all new franchisees. Do not, at first, attempt to create your constitutions EX NIHILO. You are not God. Not yet. Remember that words are YOUR FRIENDS. They've been used by others and can be used AGAIN AND AGAIN, adapting to new situations. Therefore, we strongly recommend that you construct your new constitution out of an existing one, using any of CU's tested transformational procedures: S+7, homonyms, lipograms, perverbs, semo-definitional expansion and so on. (Please review the concatenation section of this employee handbook). Using these handy shortcuts, you can construct an ABSOLUTELY NEW constitution that will delight your clients and perhaps even serve their needs. Such a transformed constitution will carry over some of the powers and rights vested in the original, in addition to generating ABSOLUTELY NEW POWERS AND RIGHTS!

88nov02 from Multatuli

Hypothetical situation. You've got a customer with mucho bucks, willing to blow his wad on the big one. So go ahead! Convene a CONSONANTAL CONGRESS and devise a CONSONANTAL CONSTITUTION. Semitic languages like Arabic are, as we all know, based on a consonantal root system. The root k-t-b yields the words "kataba" (to write), "kitaab" (book), "kaatib" (clerk), and, in certain written texts, you are only given this root. Context suggest which word is indicated. Our CONSTITUTIONS UNLIMITED CONSONANTAL MODEL consists of just such a chain of vowel-less roots.

What's the gimmick? Simple. Your Constitution asserts its power over B-R-D. Do you mean warm-blooded, feathered vertebrates with wings? A woman about to be married? The children in one family? A vulgar woman? A long, flat slab of sawed lumber? That which is hidden in the earth? A staple food made from flour or meal mixed with a liquid, usually combined with a leavening agent? A genetic strain or type of organism having consistent and recognizable inherited characteristics? One of an ancient Celtic order of singing poets who composed and recited verses on the history of their tribes? A ribbon or band used to fasten the hair? A tapered nail with a small head or a slight side projection instead of a head? Someone overcome by the dullness of his or her surroundings? That which is exposed to view? Rubbed away by friction? Or whatever occurs outside the boundaries of one's own country?
In fact, BY MERELY SPECIFYING THE ROOT, YOU CAN CLAIM POWER OVER ALL OF THESE!!— That is, over BIRD, BRIDE, BROOD, BROAD, BOARD, the BURIED, BREAD, BREED, BARD, BRAID, BRAD, BORED, anything BARED, anything you ABRADE, anything ABROAD!!!

▌89feb02 from Interior Boy

Another great sideline is PUNCTUATION. A guy walks in, he already has his constitution, and he thinks, now I really need an amendment. He really wants one, he's motivated, you're motivated, you give him the full treatment, but after it's all said and done, you both realize that he can't honestly afford even a minor amendment right now. Is this a lost sale? HELL NO! Sell him some punctuation! You can't amend with it, but you can at least play around with nuances in the existing text—with surprising results sometimes. Through EFFECTIVE SALESMANSHIP you can send the guy out the door HAPPY. You'll be happy too, 'cause the mark-up on punctuation is so high it oughta be illegal. Your constitution nerd type of customer scarfs it up, too. He's got a twenty-two article doc, fifty-seven amendments, but he can't leave it alone. You know the type. (And you love him!) He'll drop in for extra punctuation once or twice a week, like clockwork, and spend the whole evening refining sentences to the point of incomprehensibility. Sooner or later, he'll mess it up so much that he junks it and comes in for a whole new constitution!▌

▌89feb10 from Multatuli

I assume our amiable entrepreneurs market a whole line of constitutions—economy to deluxe models. You pay more and more is constituted. The least expensive model—a rather flimsy constitution—lacks enduring force or binding power. Good in limited circumstances, specified in tiny print. Liable to self-abrogate at any moment—like when you wave it before an angry lynch mob. Perhaps the tiny print "delegates power (to) freely disregard the values that moved (its enactment)." Or, there's a clause that delegates unspecified powers for whatever the future might invite.

The deluxe model, now . . . The Top of the Line . . . well, no one has ever bought one. It's existence as a prototype is only rumored. We're talking about the ultimate Constitution—or, rather, (same thing) the Constitution Machine. This baby is totally binding. Self-amending. Divine force. Ontological writing. This is the word made flesh. The word that makes that angry lynch mob cringe, melt away. This Constitution Machine would convert your own particular needs or preferences into The Law. And so Pierre and François, after years of diligent research in the Library of Babel, are perhaps on the verge of domesticating the infinite.▌

89feb22 from The Vice Editor

From: Table of Contents, Franchisee's Confidential Operations Manual
Section VII Product Enforcement: Keeping Our Competitive Edge

A. Image Maintenance: Bad Press and How to Deal With it
B. Competitive Analysis Chart: How We Stack Up Against the
    Competition
C. Mano a Mano with "The Other Guy:" Winning Jurisdictional Disputes
D. Emergencies: How to Handle Accidents, Revolutions, Authority
    Failures
E. Security: Protection of the Physical Premises; Personal Safety;
    Industrial Espionage

89mar17 from invented god

Generic device. The second reading, or the "shooter in the margin."
First text. The franchisee's kit. Typeset. Post-Gutenberg.
Text two. The scrawl in the margins. Handwritten. Pre-Gutenberg. A
nagging, insistent voice that argues with the text it reads and opens up
a second, a third, infinite readings. It takes words, plays with them,
questions. The voice, perhaps of some would-be franchiser driven to
rage by the manifest unreality of his or her prospects of success. A
voice alternately lucid and crankish, profound and dangerously para-
noid. Making short, intermittent appearances in the early pages; growing more visibly desperate and long-winded in the later parts, until
these scrawls in the margin parallel the text.

So you can read the text. And, simultaneously, read it through the eyes
of the second reader—the "shooter in the margin," always about to
snap in the cartridge clip and adjust the scope, having scrawled these
comments in the margin as a kind of last testament before embarking
on the deed which will be his or her definitive act of literary criticism
and, against which, Pierre and François and all of the employees of the
Constitutions Unlimited Chain have been vainly preparing defenses.

Astonish Us!

"Is there life after literature?" asked the preface to the printed *Invisible Seattle's Omnia* magazine of 1985.

The answer is yes. The experience of IN.S.OMNIA and the hundreds of other similar projects under way leaves all readers and writers with a choice. Either they can continue to consider writing and reading to be entirely contained in their favorite bookstore, or they can include the writing accessible by modem and found in the *wunderkammer* of the world. They can choose to acknowledge or reject the unclassified, marginal experiences of reading and writing that already fill their odd moments.

We as in.s.omniacs are used to living in such a permeable world. We have a taste for it, and we're thirsty for more. We have offered our few experiences. Now you are implored to come and astonish us!

Writers of criticism and analysis!

Let us see the world of linkage the way people use it! Teach us to enjoy combinations of culture. Teach us to connect events that occur over time, to connect work in multiple media. If the intimacies of Anais Nin's diaries are unveiled by being published over decades in increasingly frank installments, isn't the timing of that process part of its effect? If filmmaker Spike Lee always writes and publishes a book with every film, don't film and book form a "project?" If the nature of some projects (the magnificent Subgeniuses, for example) is participation rather than exhibition, isn't it time for a new critical perspective—notes from the user, rather than the observer?

Voltaire died convinced that his eternal glory rested on his great tragic dramas, dramas that are rarely read and even more rarely produced today. The letters, the essays—mere journalism! Dated jottings of topical interest only! How often have works that were considered "recreational" eclipsed a writer's "serious" productions in the eyes of history! "Are the novels of today," asks in.s.omniac Multatuli (IN.S.OMNIA 1991), "the 'Voltaire's tragedies' of the 21st century?"

Let's see critical thought put to the "experience design" of parties and other private cultural events. A tame example: certain Chicago in.s.omniacs plot what they call $8^1/_2$ events that strive for a systematic overeducation of the senses—multiple televisions, books, books on tape, radios—pouring into bodies charged with nothing but coffee. Their starting point is the psychological finding that humans can usefully hold a maximum of seven things in their minds at any one time. The name $8^1/_2$ was chosen not only to indicate the attempt to push that limit, but because it already has a meaning and connotations (Fellini's film). Reusing the name "overloads" it with connections. The $8^1/_2$-ers are known for their great love of *Finnegans Wake,* that giant Irish rec room filled with radios, TVs, books, turntables, and cassette decks, all blasting away.

Compositors and Designers!

Let's see paper printouts that better correspond to the discoveries of the electronic realm, that translate and extend these methods into the print medium.

Writers of software, Sysops, Literary Contractors!

Let's see software with personality, even obnoxious personality, such as the word processor envisioned by in.s.omniac David Zank (IN.S.OMNIA 1986). This program would do more than beep while it automatically changed a misspelled word (as some already do). This program would actually reach in and change a word you had written, automatically tinker with your prose, refuse to print certain words, deflect the course of your text, challenge you to overcome certain obstacles. Let's see a word processor that really *processes*, like a food processor!

Let's see literary essays in the form of software, like the old IN.S.OMNIA idea of *The Ameliorator*, a program that would use compound Oulipean algorithms to rescue inadequate writing. "Garbage in, beauty out!" goes the slogan. "Is your home one of the millions that contains a box of incomplete short stories somewhere on a shelf? A notebook of old poems? A half-finished novel? *The Ameliorator* will perform an automatic literary makeover! *The Ameliorator*, thanks to the latest literary engineering, combines your fragments with others unlike them to build texts of extraordinary luster. We stand beside our motto: There Are No Bad Books (IN.S.OMNIA 1986)."

Let's finally see that bulletin board that will capture the rhythm of composition—the pauses, false starts, erasures. Imagine a user signing on under a pseudonym and copying a message, already written out in longhand, onto the system—putting in false pauses, fake corrections, just for effect. Imagine watching a replay, like a player piano roll, of Proust writing. Imagine a scholar, working from manuscripts, recording a facsimile piano roll of Proust writing.

Let's see bulletin boards with startling links to unseen aspects of life—public writing receptacles around the world, links to the working computers of weird magazines and weirder art studios. Imagine a contract that would require your favorite contemporary writer to write a text (intended for print publication elsewhere) on a machine that was connected, live, to your bulletin board system, twenty-four hours a day. If you called up and the writer was eating or sleeping, all you would see would be the last page of what she had written, sitting motionless on the screen. If she went on vacation, that page would stay for days. But what if by chance on a hot, irritable night, boredom drove you to your terminal and you happened to glance in her room and find her working? Feverish paragraphs interrupted by five-minute lapses. Is she pacing? Making coffee? Consulting books? Which books? You watch her come up with sentences that are brilliant or a lame parody of herself. Are there others watching, or are you the only one? Is the knowledge that you are there, or might be, changing the text? Is it therefore partly *your* text?

Let's see bulletin boards that offer services such as the "Hugaphone" (an idea in Krueger's *Artificial Reality* (1983, 232) for the solace of long-distance lovers. A Krueger bed would use tiny motors in the mattress and inexpensive packet-switching telecommunications to create a warm, raised form to indicate where the other person is sleeping. The forms would move as the two move.

Let's see solutions to the distribution problems of the traditional print publishing industry. Can we beat warehousing costs by long-distance relay of books in electronic form, coupled with local printing on demand?

Let's see a "Books While You Wait" booth. Modeled on the tiny photo finishing huts that proliferated in the '80s, "Books While You Wait" could offer printing on demand of books from a huge on-line library. "Why don't you have a little snack over at Mr. Donuts, sir. Your book will be ready in fifteen minutes."

Let's see a fully automated "Jukebooks." A Jukebooks would be a honking, flashing, Wurlitzer-style credenza that holds gigabytes of messages on laser disk and sports a showy laser printer. A passerby flips through the catalog, inserts the payment, and watches while the pages roll out into the tray.

Writers, readers, users! Meet us at the invisible rendezvous! "You," as the map says, "are here."

References

Addison, Joseph. 1876. *The Spectator*. Edited by George Washington Greene. 2 vols. Philadelphia: J. B. Lippincott & Co.

Bantock, Nick. 1992. *Sabine's Notebook*. San Francisco: Chronicle Books.

Between C and D, Post-Coital Lower East Side Fiction Magazine. Volume 6 Number 1 (Summer).

Bolter, Jay David. 1991. *Writing Space: The Computer, Hypertext, and the History of Writing*. Hillsdale, N.J.: Lawrence Erlbaum.

Books in Print. 1948–. New York: R. R. Bowker Co.

Borges, Jorge Luis. 1962. The Garden of Forking Paths. In *Labyrinths, Selected Stories & Other Writings*. New York: New Directions.

Calvino, Italo. 1976. *The Castle of Crossed Destinies*. Translated by William Weaver. New York: Harcourt Brace Jovanovich. Originally published as *Il castello dei destini incrociati*. Franco Maria Ricci editore. 1969.

———. 1981. *If on a Winter's Night a Traveler*. Translated by William Weaver. New York: Harcourt Brace Jovanovich. Originally published as *Se una notte d'inverno un viaggiatore*. Torino: Giulio Einaudi editore s.p.a. 1979.

———. 1984. *Collezione di sabbia*. Garzanti Editore. Translation here by Rob Wittig.

———. 1986. *The Uses of Literature*. Translated Patrick Creagh. New York: Harcourt Brace Jovanovich.

Carkeek, Janet. 1990. *Carkeek's Pocket Guide to Plywood Veneer Grades*. New York: Feature Gallery.

CCI (Centre de Création Industrielle). 1985. *Epreuves d'écriture*. (Collaborative writing on an electronic network.) Paris: Editions du Centre Georges Pompidou.

Certeau, Michel de. 1984. *The Practice of Everyday Life*. Translated by Steven Rendall. Berkeley: University of California Press.

Coffy, Didier. 1985–. *Invisible Seattle*. A suite of publications, manuscripts, drawings, paintings, sculptures, and performances. Paris and elsewhere: Didier Coffy.

Csikszentmihalyi, Mihaly. 1990. *Flow: the Psychology of Optimal Experience*. New York. Harper & Row.

Darnton, Robert. 1979. *The Business of the Enlightenment: A Publishing History of the Encyclopédie 1755–1800*. Cambridge, Mass.: The Belknap Press of Harvard University Press.

Deleuze, Gilles, and Félix Guattari. 1987. *A Thousand Plateaus, Capitalism and Schizophrenia*. Translated by Brian Massumi. Minneapolis: University of Minnesota Press.

Eco, Umberto. 1989. *Foucault's Pendulum*. Translated by William Weaver. New York: Harcourt Brace Jovanovich.

Ede, Lisa, and Andrea Lunsford. 1990. *Singular Texts/Plural Authors, Perspectives on Collaborative Writing*. Carbondale, Ill.: Southern Illinois University Press.

Fairpipe, Jessica (collective pseudonym of Invisible Seattle). 1981–1983. Spawning Grounds; or, A Romance of a Woman Alone in the Frozen North. *Voice of the Singles Life*.

Fitch, Noel Riley. 1983. *Sylvia Beach and the Lost Generation*. New York: W. W. Norton & Company.

Gunderloy, Michael A., and Cari Goldberg, eds. *Factsheet Five*. 1991. Number 42. Rensselaer, NY: Mike Gunderloy.

Haywood, Ian. 1987. *Faking It: Art and the Politics of Forgery*. New York: St. Martin's Press.

Humphries, David. 1981. One Life to Sorta Live, Invisible Seattle Strikes Back. *The Daily* (*University of Washington*).

IN.S.OMNIA [electronic bulletin board]. 1983–. First central processing unit and digital memory, Seattle. Second central processing unit and digital memory, Chicago. The extent of paper archives is unknown; in theory all users are able to print copies of their on-line sessions. Citations for this book are drawn principally from the paper archives of Rob Wittig, Lynn Martinelli, Philip Wohlstetter, and Tom Grothus.

IN.S.OMNIA Print Outs 1. 1987. *The Plan for Invisible America: More Than a Game—More Than a Novel, a Stupendous, Computer-Based, Bilingual, Transatlantic, Collaborative, History-Making Project*. Literary Contractors and Lead Writers, Lynn Martinelli and Rob Wittig. Paris: IN.S.OMNIA Print Outs.

IN.S.OMNIA Print Outs 2. 1987. *Prospectus for &ncyclopedia 1: An Illuminated Fictionary/ Fictionnaire Illuminé*. Literary Contractors and Lead Writers, Rob Wittig and Didier Coffy. Paris: IN.S.OMNIA Print Outs.

IN.S.OMNIA Print Outs 3. 1990. *The Andrew Salt: A Series of Messages Left on the Electronic Bulletin Board IN.S.OMNIA in March and April of 1987*. Literary Contractor and compiler, Rob Wittig. Designer, Ed Schweitzer. Chicago: IN.S.OMNIA Print Outs.

IN.S.OMNIA Print Outs 4. 1990 (reprint of a 1986 project). *The Library of Borges: A Chain Letter Novel*. Literary Contractor and Lead Writer, Philip Wohlstetter. Designer, Joanne Aono. Chicago: IN.S.OMNIA Print Outs.

IN.S.OMNIA Print Outs 5. 1991. *Code of the Literary Duel*. Literary Contractor and Lead Writer, Rob Wittig. Designer, DECODE. Chicago: IN.S.OMNIA Print Outs.

Invisible Seattle. 1980a. *Make Room for Dada*. Poster. Seattle: Invisible Seattle.

———. 1980b. *The Daily Zeitgeist: The Official Publication of Invisible Seattle*. Seattle: Bumbershoot Literary Arts Committee.

———. 1980c. *The Map of Invisible Seattle*. Designers, Joy Winchell and Kathleen Skeels.

———. 1981. *The Daily Zeitgeist: The Official Publication of Invisible Seattle*. Seattle: Bumbershoot Literary Arts Committee.

———. 1982. *The Daily Zeitgeist: The Official Publication of Invisible Seattle*. Seattle: Bumbershoot Literary Arts Committee.

———. 1983a. *The Daily Zeitgeist: The Official Publication of Invisible Seattle*. Seattle: Bumbershoot Literary Arts Committee.

———. 1983b. *Attention all ___! Your ____ is needed now!* Poster. Seattle: Invisible Seattle.

———. 1984. *The Daily Zeitgeist: The Official Publication of Invisible Seattle*. Seattle: Bumbershoot Literary Arts Committee.

———. 1987. *Invisible Seattle: The Novel of Seattle, by Seattle*. Seattle: Function Industries Press. Also known as Version 5.2 "The Six by Nine Version." (Version 1.0 "The Database" All the disks, tapes, pages, drafts, maps, and boxes of raw material, 1983. Version 2.0 "The Version of Four Days" First draft completed on the morning of August 6, 1983 at the Bumbershoot Festival. Version 3.0 "The Mayor's Version" Recompiled and presented to Seattle Mayor Charles Royer, September, 1983. Version 3.5 "The Radio Version" Broadcast serially on KUOW-FM, Seattle, October 17 through November 7, 1983. Version 4.0 "The Illustrated Version" Figures and subheads completed, Spring 1984. Version 5.0 "The Visible Invisible" Extracts. Seattle: Function Industries Press, 1984.)

Invisible Seattle's Omnia [IN.S.OMNIA]. 1985. Number 1. Seattle: Invisible Seattle Projects in association with Function Industries Press.

Kleiser, Grenville. 1917. *Fifteen Thousand Useful Phrases: A Practical Handbook of Pertinent Expressions, Striking Similes, Literary, Commercial, Conversational, and Oratorical Terms, for the Embellishment of Speech and Literature, and the Improvement of the Vocabulary of Those Persons Who Read, Write, and Speak English*. New York: Funk & Wagnalls Company.

Krueger, Myron W. 1983. *Artificial Reality*. Reading, Mass.: Addison-Wesley.

———. 1991. *Artificial Reality Second Edition*. Reading, Mass.: Addison-Wesley.

Landow, George P. 1992. *Hypertext: The Convergence of Contemporary Critical Theory and Technology*. Baltimore: The Johns Hopkins University Press.

Manuscript 1991. Three pages thought to be in the hand of James Winchell. Archives of Rob Wittig.

Manuscript 1992. Scrap. Archives of Rob Wittig.

Mathews, Harry. 1991. *Immeasurable Distances: The Collected Essays*. Venice, Calif.: The Lapis Press.

Motte, Warren F. Jr. 1986. *Oulipo: A Primer of Potential Literature*. Lincoln: University of Nebraska Press.

O'Rourke, P. J., ed. 1978. *National Lampoon Sunday Newspaper Parody*. New York: National Lampoon, Inc.

Perec, Georges. 1969. *La Disparition*. Paris: Denoël.

————. 1974. *Espèces d'espaces*. Paris: Editions Galilée. (Translation here by Rob Wittig.)

————. 1978. "Tentative de description de choses vues au carrefour Mabillon le 19 mai 1978." Atelier de Création radiophonique, no. 381.

————. 1985. *Penser/Classer*. Paris: Hachette. (Translation here by Rob Wittig.)

————. 1987. *Life A User's Manual*. Translated by David Bellos. Boston: David R. Godine. Originally published as *La Vie mode d'emploi*. Paris: Hachette, 1978.

————. 1990. *Things. A Story of the Sixties*. Translated by David Bellos. Boston: David. R. Godine. Originally published as *Les Choses. Une histoire des annés soixante*. Paris: René Julliard, 1965.

Perkins, Stephen, plagiarist. Anti-copyright 1989. *Festival of Plagiarism*. San Francisco: Plagiarist Press.

Phillips, Tom. 1980. *A Humument: A Treated Victorian Novel*. First Revised Edition. London: Thames and Hudson Ltd.

Phonic. Undated. Home-compiled cassette with laser-printed label listing names of bands. Boston.

Queneau, Raymond. 1961. *Cent Mille Milliards de poèmes*. Paris: Gallimard.

Robbe-Grillet, Alain. 1953. *Les Gommes*. Paris: Les Editions de Minuit.

Rosen, Kay. 1982. *Lines on Lines*. Gary, Indiana: Kay Rosen.

Saporta, Marc. 1962. *Composition No. 1*. Paris: Éditions du Seuil.

Sitbon, Guy. 1987. Minitel. *Le Nouvel Observateur* (January).

Spence, Kristin. 1993. If You're Headed to Rochester for Montage '93. *Wired* (July/August).

Sproull, Lee, and Sara Kiesler. 1991. Computers, Networks and Work. *Scientific American* (September).

Stang, Rev. Ivan, ed. 1990. *Three-Fisted Tales of "Bob," Short Stories in the Subgenius Mythos*. New York: Fireside.

Stillinger, Jack. 1991. *Multiple Authorship and the Myth of Solitary Genius*. New York: Oxford University Press.

Subgenius Foundation. 1981. *Repent! Quit Your Job! Slack Off!* Pamphlet. Dallas: The Subgenius Foundation.

———. 1983. *The Book of the Subgenius, Lunatic Prophecies for the Coming Weird Times.* New York: McGraw Hill.

Trebay, Guy. 1993. Cross-Dresser Dreams, How RuPaul, a Black Man in a Platinum Wig and Platform Heels, Captured the Imagination of Mainstream Pop Culture. *The New Yorker*, 22 March, 49–54.

Universal Pictures. 1970. Advertising Publicity Promotion, *Anne of the Thousand Days*. Los Angeles: Universal Pictures Ltd.

Wendy and Tom. 1987. *Couple Weds in Bizarre Ceremony*. Xeroxed booklet. Seattle.

Wittig, Rob. 1983. Rules of the Game. *The Daily Zeitgeist*.

Wohlstetter, Philip. 1980. The Search for Invisible Seattle. *The Daily Zeitgeist*.

———. 1981a. The Search for Invisible Seattle. *The Daily Zeitgeist*.

———. 1981b. The Prosecution of Tom Robbins, as Performed by Invisible Seattle. *The Weekly*. 16–22 September, 1981.

———. 1983. *Guest Writers' Guidelines*. Typescript. Seattle: Invisible Seattle.

Wohlstetter, Philip, and Rob Wittig. 1984. Invisible Seattle, Function Follows Fiction: Taking Over a City by Hypnotic Suggestion. *High Performance*, issue 27.

Wright, Diane. 1981. Even Robbins Gets the Blues. *The Everett Herald*, 8 September.

Credits

STORYTELLERS

LIARS

JOKESTERS

SOPHISTS

ADVENTURERS

"HOMER"
The Odyssey, The Iliad
(collaborative)

PHILOSOPHERS

CAVE PAINTERS
Potters

GEOGRAPHERS

Archilochus

Memories

Mediterranean Shipping

"Truth"
Heliodorus

Ovid

Clay

PTOLEMY
Cosmographia

Ossian

ROMAN ROADS
(Bureaucratic Administration)

1001 Nights
(collaborative)

PAPYRUS

Stone

Pausanius
Guide to Greece

Bayeaux Tapestry

b. Albion 216 A.D.,
d. Invisible Seattle 284 A.D.

ISIDORE OF SEVILLE
Etymologies

Chretien de Troyes

Parchment

Religious & Military Administration

Robert Greene

Pilgrimages

MARCO POLO
Voyages

DANTE
Divine Comedy

RABELAIS

Lazarillo de Tormes

Walnut Gall
Ink

ANTONIO
PIGAFETTA
Journal

Catherine
de Rambouillet

Aphra Behn

Licensed Book Sellers

POST STATION NETWORK

DEFOE
Robinson Crusoe

Meindert Hobbema

Voltaire
English Letters

Gibbon
Rise and Fall of the Roman Empire

Chatterton

Tristram Shandy
Sentimental Journey

Sterne

Art & Novelty Dealers

Stage Coaches

Sir Walter Scott

James McPherson
"Ossian's" Works

Cleland
French Letters

COLONIALISM

Thomas Hopkins Gallaudet

POST OFFICES
State & Private

R. L. Stevenson

Brothers Wright

International Expos

Verne

MUSEUMS

TELEGRAPH

Lord Baden Powell

Maria Montessori

JAMES JOYCE
Ulysses
Finnegans Wake

Public Libraries

L. ARMSTRONG

James Gould Cozzens

Mayakovsky

HENRY MORTON STANLEY
How I Found Livingstone in Central Africa

Victoria's Golden Jubilee

Eiffel Tower

Alaska-Yukon-Pacific Exposition

ROUSSEL

H.D.

WPA's U.S. Guidebooks

J. C. Onetti

Michelin Guides

Alfred "Joey" Perlès

MICHEL FOUCAULT

SITUATIONISTS

Seattle World's Fair

Thor Heyerdahl
Kon Tiki

BORGES

Jacques Cousteau

Robbe-Grillet

John Clellon Holmes

Bumbershoot Arts Festival, Seattle

TED JOANS

Angela Carter

Gunnar Gunnarson

Knut Hamsun

SHERWOOD ANDERSON

DADA

Surrealists

Exquisite Corpse
Nadja
Trial of Barrès
Manifestoes
Paysan de Paris

QUENEAU

Oulipo

PEREC

MATHEWS

ROUBAUD

Suzanne Lacey

Jean (Hans) Arp & Sophie Tauber Arp

Picabia

DUCHAMP

MAN RAY

LEE MILLER

Calder
Circus

Wodehouse

MODOTTI

CALVINO

Vance Packard

RAILROAD

TELEPHONE

Private Cars

Highways

Carroll Shelby

Air Mail

Les Paul

MATTA

WOUK

Dossier Detective Novels

Monique Wittig

CONSUMER ELECTRONICS

ECO

BROADCAST RADIO & TELEVISION

Apollo VIII

Vosnesensky

George Martin

Video Games

PERSONAL COMPUTERS

Eno

Invisible Seattle

founded, 1979

MICHEL BUTOR
Mobile

Nancy Graves

Philip Wohlstetter
James Winchell
Jean Sherrard
Larry Stone

Selma Diamond

THE OFF THE WALL PLAYERS

Starbuck's™ Coffee

Mary Machala
Coby Scheldt

Joy Winchell

Claus Oldenburg

Clair Colquitt's sculpture

FRED FOREST
Stock Exchange of the Imaginary

15,000 Useful Phrases

Erin Peterson
Linda Smith
Roxanne Jantz
Tim Detmer
Paul McKee
Cindy Smith

CIRCA

Guide to Mysterious Paris

John Siscoe
Joseph Guppy

Literary Cabaret Events

Steve Ramage
David Kline
Paul Loper
Norah Nepas
Clifford Hunt

Fred Moody
David Humphries

Jesse Burnstein
Penny Lee
Bob Sawatzski
Claudia Jones

Elliott Bay Café

Arnold "Mucusless" Ehret
Kenward Elmslie
Jon Persson
Bob Chrysafouli
Michael Meade
Toca

Trial of Tom Robbins

Spawning Grounds

Janet Skeels
Charles Cross
John Jordan
Kathleen Skeels

Paul Dorpat

Fabian Lloyd

BARTHES

Rob Wittig
Philip Lamb
Lynn Martinelli
Christine Charters
Paul Cabarga

Invisible Seattle City Council Meeting

John Shaw
Ann S. Price
Nikolai Stavrogin
Allison Loris

Bogdana Carpenter
Christina Wohlstetter
Andy Stein
Brad Caldart
Dale Goodson
Lisa Ravenholt
Donald Barthelme
Ryan Whitney
Erica Helm
Layra Teeters
Virginia Galvin

DIGITAL DATA TRANSMISSION

TELETEXT

VIDEOTEX

MINITEL

JEAN-FRANÇOIS LYOTARD
Bernard Steigler
LES IMMATÉRIAUX

"Big Phone" Bill appears courtesy of
Tamper Proof Seals/Lawn Dart Lobotomy
Big Stupid Records™

JACQUES DERRIDA

David Hockney
Gilbert & George
Vaughn Grylls

Herb Caen

Warren Motte

CHURCH OF THE SUBGENIUS

C-Span Network

The Weather Channel

RÉDA BENSMAIA

The Novel Project

Clark Humphrey
L.L.
Ricky Rankin
Reidar Dittmann, Jr.

Claudia Royal
Walt Briem
Eileen Briem
Robin on 'cello &
back-up vocals
Lori Larsen
Rex McDowell

Ted Holzman
Clair Colquitt
Joyce Moty
David Zank
Tom Grothus

IN.S.OMNIA

CLAIR COLQUITT
GYDA FOSSLAND

Lex Station Borges

The Plan for Invisible America

Prospectus for &ncyclopedia 1

Linda Lewis
Monica Carpenter
Roger Hagen
Kathryn Thompson
Larry Lance

Jeff Baron
Valerie Bystrom
David Willingham
Al Snapp
Dexter Buhl
Patty Shaw

HENRY ART GALLERY
Engines of Desire

Lisa Ravenholt
Jane Blair
Kalin Huffman
Nick Vroman
Howard Lev

Mary Lydon
SYDNEY LÉVY
Ted Pope

Tama Janowitz

MICHEL DE CERTEAU

M. Kasper

Paul Zelevansky

DIDIER COFFY

A.C. Milan

Le Petit Berry

National Lampoon's High School Yearbook Parody

ULMER

MYRON KRUEGER

Robert Darnton

Hudson

The Anonymous Museum of Chicago©

STEVE LAFRENIERE

Petite fabrique de littérature
Alain Duchesne, Thierry Leguay

Margeurite Bonnet, Ed.
André Breton, Oeuvres Complètes

Lush

Lenses by Panavision™

LIGATURE INC.   Orbital   John Landrigan
Josef Godlewski
Richard Anderson   Mary Mellow   The Orb

Philip Wohlstetter   Nanine Hutchinson
Scholar

APPLE COMPUTERS   Black Dog Productions

The pages of this book were   Jeremy Langford   Mike Burton
digitally remastered on a
Macintosh II ci   FRAM™ Oil Filters   Mark Rattin

Mary Crittenden

others who inspired ➡

Constitutions Unlimited

The Andrew Salt

The Library of Borges

Code of the Literary Duel

Invisible Rendezvous

Wesleyan University Press
TERRY COCHRAN
SUZANNA TAMMINEN

Rob Wittig   Lynn Martinelli
Literary Contractor   ***Improvisator***
Lead Writer   ***Diagram Design***

KAYPRO COMPUTERS
This book was drafted on a
Kaypro II
with 64 Mighty K of memory

Mont Blanc, Parker, Waterman

others we read ➡

The Mode of Information
Mark Poster

Kay Rosen   Ed Schweitzer

Joanne Aono

Steve Dahl

Chet Chitchat

L'auteur et ses doubles
Abdelfattah Kilito

Jay David Bolter   Eddie Abler

The Good Outdoorsman Show

Stuart Moulthrop   George Landow

ROBERT SEIGLE   DECODE
Page Design
STEVE LYONS
JOHN JENKINS

Paul Cabarga
Clark Humphrey   DJ Derrick Carter
Tom Grothus
Gyda Fossland   Mike Piper   Precor™

Tony Klaasen

others who contributed

182 ➡

Index

Actual Size ('nym), 17
Addison, Joseph, 4, 37
Anderson, Chester, 131
Ajar, Emile, 152
Alembert, Jean Le Rond d', 114
Ameliorator, The, 170
Artaud, Antonin, 3
Anne of the Thousand Days, 4
Ashbery, John, 89

background noise ('nym), 158
Bad Reader, The ('nym), 92–93
Bantock, Nick, 4
Baudrillard, Jean, 131
Beach, Sylvia, 137
Beaumont, Francis, 137
BeLong ('nym), 12
Benny, Jack, 95
Between C and D, 4
"Big Phone" Bill ('nym), 5, 10, 134, 161
Blanchot, Maurice, 131
Bogue, Vergil, 43
"Books While You Wait," 170–171
Bolter, Jay David, 87, 114
Borges, Jorge Luis, 43, 111–112, 116
Boulez, Pierre, 131
Braffort, Paul, 73
Breton, André, 137
Bunny, Lady, 154
Burrow, J. A., 141
Butler, Rhett ('nym), 151
Bystander # One ('nym), 156

Caeiro, Alberto, 152

Cabarga, Paul, 20
Calvino, Italo
    "if a new world were discovered," 1
    If on a Winter's Night a Traveler, 73
    Invisible Cities and Invisible Seattle, 42
    member of Oulipo, 72
    multiple constraint books, 110
    The Castle of Crossed Destinies, 88–89
Campos, Alvaro de, 152
Carkeek, Janet, 4
Carpet Sample ('nym), 5
Certeau, Michel de, 128–130
Chumleigh, Reverend, 41
Clair ('nym), 79
Coffy, Didier, 119
Coller, Ken ('nym), 79
Colquitt, Clair
    brings first computer to Invisible Seattle
        meeting, 69
    early drawing for his Scheherezade II,
        51
    and In.s.omnium, 115
Commins, Saxe, 137
Conrad, Joseph, 137
Constitutions Unlimited
    described, 111
    fragments from the development of, 159
Correct, Eugene ('nym)
    dead and selling cars, 19
    in R'evolution Room, 78
    kills self, 17
    on "self" and 'nyms, 148
    on Zyzzyzzyzyzwa, 24
cranky ('nym), 19

Csikszentmihalyi, Mihaly, 133
Cultural activists
    defined, 3
    and technology, 6

Dada, *x*
Daily Zeitgeist, The, 43
Darnton, Robert, 114
Davis, Vaginal Creme, 154
Deleuze, Gilles, 154, 155
Delgado, Pienso ('nym)
    on scrolling, 19
    upset, 17
DeNiro, Robert, 153
Desnos, Robert, 154
Desperado # One ('nym), 150, 156
Desperado # 3 ('nym), 156
Diderot, Denis, 114
Dorpat, Paul, 41
Drummond, Dr. Philo, 147
Duchamp, Marcel, 72

Eco, Umberto, 5, 131
Ede, Lisa, 135, 138–139

Fabbri, Paolo, 131
Faulkner, William, 137
Feature Gallery, 4
Festival of Plagiarism. *See* Perkins, Stephen
Fielding, Cyrus T., 102
Fitch, Noel Riley, 137
Fitzgerald, F. Scott, 137
Ford, Ford Madox, 137
Foreperson ('nym), 131–132
Fletcher, John, 137
Freud, Sigmund, 130, 154

Gardner, Carl, 40
Gary, Romain, 152
Genius
    and crediting issue, 138, 139–140
    dismissal of occasional writers by, 143
    God in the guise of, *x*
    Homer as, *ix*
    vs. conception of common man, 130
Gesualdo, Carlo, 3
Goldberg, Cari, 4

Grothus ('nym)
    fishhook quote, 2
    "I am a Livingstone," 108
    texts culled for "Naive Writing
        Room," 22–23
Guapo, Rico E. ('nym), 19
Guattari, Félix, 154, 155
Gunderloy, Mike, 4
Guppy, Joe, 40
GUZMAN-CHANG, MEI LAN ('nym), 149

Hapless User ('nym), 151
Haywood, Ian, 141
Hemingway, Ernest, 137
Homer, ix, 137
Humphrey, Clark ('nym)
    Constitutions Unlimited, 162, 164
    in "R'evolution Room," 80
    on landmarks, 44
    on Zyzzyzyzyzyzwa, 14
Hypertext
    definition, 94
    "hypertext novel" as transitional
        term, 107
    interaction in, 113
    The Novel Project as physical, 94
IN.S.OMNIA
    analogy for changing world, 8
    basic description, 2
    early goals of, 21
    development of, 7
    genres of rooms on, 107–108
    roles of users on, 141–143
    technical description of, 16
    technology includes phone calls and
        letters, 26
    users' descriptions of, 18
    welcome message of, 16
In.s.omniacs
    defined, 3
    other lives of, 8
    we meet again behind the mask, 9
In.s.omnium, 114, 100–101
Interior Boy ('nym), 98, 149, 166
invented god ('nym), 162, 167
Invisible America. *See Plan for Invisible
    America, The*

Invisibles, x, 6. *See also* in.s.omniacs
Invisible Seattle
    activities 1980, 42, 45
    City Council Meeting 1982, 48
    group, 6
    open meetings, 126
    renaming streets, 42, 46
    self-described history, 31
    three zones of, 35
    Wohlstetter on foundations of, *ix*
Invisible Seattle: The Novel of Seattle, by
    Seattle. See Novel Project, The
Invisible Seattle's Omnia
    back cover of, 6
    nature of IN.S.OMNIA, 21
    Notes for a New Medium, 84–85
    reader and writer roles, 20–21
Invisible America. See Plan for Invisible
    America, The
Jackson, Fertile Latoyah, 154
Jarry, Alfred, 3
Joyce, James, 137
"Jukebooks," 171

Kauffman, Andy, 3
Kiesler, Sara, 20
Klein, David, 40
Kleiser, Grenville, 71
Krueger, Myron W.
    "Hugaphone," 170
    Videoplace concept, 27
Kruger, Barbara, 131

LaMotta, Jake, 154
Landow, George, 71
Lee, Spike, 168
Le Lionnais, François, 71
Les Immatériaux, 4
Letterman, David, 147
Lex Station Borges
    Atlas facsimiles, 122–123
    described, 115–116
    photographs, 97, 123
Library of Borges, The, 111–112, 116
Lipogram, 73
Literary Contractor, 141

Literary Workers
    data gathering, 64, 65
    motivations of, 66–67
    photographed in action, 52–63
    Wohlstetter on, *x*
Lunsford, Andrea, 135, 138–139

mahoney, liz ('nym), 146
Mailer, Norman, 89
Mallarmé, Stéphane, *xi*
Map of Invisible Seattle, The
    analysis of, 43
    illustration, 32
    unveiled, 42
marquis d'maypo ('nym), 146
Mathews, Harry
    multiple constraint books, 109
    Oulipo, definition of, 71–72
    potential literature, 72–73
    PPPP (Mathews Perfectible Parody &
        Pastiche Procedure), 108–109
McBride, Tom ('nym), 146
Mehitabel ('nym), 25, 78, 146
Message (as basic unit of IN.S.OMNIA), 86–88
Minitel, 26, 104
Miss Scarlett's Letter, 111
Motte, Warren, 72
Multatuli ('nym)
    aristocratic and democratic interests on
        IN.S.OMNIA, 129
    basic principles of a "project," 110
    Chilean censorship, 23
    Constitutions Unlimited, 161, 162,
        165, 166
    "No talking about writing, only
        writing," 96
    novels as Voltaire's tragedies, 169
    scrolling, 19
    storing rhythms, 18
    wanting to write differently, 23
    Zyzzyzyzyzwa, 24–25
Murray, Arthur T. ('nym), 24

N+7, 72
National Lampoon's Sunday Newspaper
    Parody, 4

"Naive Writing Room," 22
Nelson, Theodor, 114
NETHER LANS ('nym), 152
Nin, Anaïs, 168
Novel Project, The, 7
    as physical hypertext, 94
    assessing everyday creativity, 132
    conclusions drawn from, 76–77, 86
    credit issue resolved, 144
    collaboration in, 139
    data gathering techniques during,
        67–69
    event at Bumbershoot Festival, 75–76
    how to credit, 136
    list of book titles with word Seattle
        in, 127
    no single version has priority in, 107
    origins as book signing, 127
    origins of, 65
    Prologue, 67–68
    structure of, 74–75
    Wohlstetter on, x
'nyms, 150

Off the Wall Players, 40
OK Corral, 110
Olson, Brent ('nym), 24
Oncle Jean ('nym), 98, 109
ONE ('nym), 20
O'Neill, Eugene, 137
Oulipo
    influence on the Novel Project, 65
    history and description, 71
our correspondent ('nym), 11

Paul, Les, 89
Perec, Georges
    La Disparition, 73
    Life A User's Manual, 73
    multiple constraint books, 109
    on writing as practice, 73
    Reading: A Socio-Physiological
        Sketch, 91–92, 95
Perkins, Maxwell, 137
Perkins, Stephen, 4
Person ('nym)
    Constitutions Unlimited, 159–160, 163,
    165

doing voices, 151–152
old and new worlds, 5
"self-centered" writing, 153
selves and control, 154–155
Pessoa, Fernando, 152
Phonic, 4
Plan for Invisible America, The
    everyday creativity in, 12, 132
    goals, 116–117
    interactivity, 113
    literary contracting in, 141
    mission to Paris, 7
    project description, 102–104
    sample advertisement, 106
    sample promotion, 120–121
Pound, Ezra, 137
Project (defined), 110
Prospectus for &ncyclopedia 1, 114–115
Proust, Marcel, 170

Queneau, Raymond, 71, 72, 73
Rabelais, François, 89
Rather, Dan ('nym), 151
Reis, Ricardo, 152
R-I-P ('nym), 91
Robbe-Grillet, Alain, 68, 131
Robbins, Tom. *See Trial of Tom Robbins*
Robinson, Mike ('nym), 80
Rogers, Kenny ('nym), 151
Rosen, Kay, 4
Rotisserie league baseball
    as conceptual model, 118–119
    as analogy to theory of selves, 155
    diagram(s), 124–125
    Didier Coffy's *Invisible Seattle* and
        Invisible Seattle as, 119
Roubaud, Jacques, 72
Roussel, Raymond, 88
Royer, Mayor Charles, 65
Ruebrick ('nym), 140
RuPaul, 147, 154

Saporta, Marc, 4
Satie, Erik, 3
Scheherezade II
    introduced, 64
    meaning of the design of, 75
    photographed, 51, 58–63

Scheldt, Coby, 40
Schmidt, Eric ('nym), 78
Sherrard, Jean, 42
Sikuan ('nym), 24
Sitbon, Guy, 26
Situationists, 45, 131
slothrop, tyrone ('nym), 146
SOUND EFFECTS ('nym), 150–151
Soupault, Phillippe, 137
Spain, Pleasant D., 40
*Spawning Grounds: or A Romance of a Woman
     Alone in the Frozen North,* 69–70
Spence, Kristin, 4
Sproul, Lee, 20
Stang, Reverend Ivan, 5
Steele, Sir Richard, 137
Stein, Andrea, 40
stick dood ('nym), 99
Stillinger, Jack, 138
Stock Exchange of the Imaginary, 66
Stone, Larry, 42
Strange Justice ('nym)
     asks about remixing *The Waste
          Land,* 89–90
     boundaries of literary and non-
          literary, 129
     on "making everyone an artist," 131
     library becoming Warner Bros.
          cartoon, 111
Subgenius, Church of the
     "audience" participation in, 168
     as "project," 118
     never breaks character, 6
     High Weirdness by Mail, 5
     Philo Drummond on publication of, 147
     "Slack off" brochure, 4
"Successful Singles Room," 109
Surrealism
     and geography, 45
     television remote control as, 90
     sommeils, 154
     Surrealist Research Bureau, 66
System Operator ('nym), 80

T'an T'u ('nym), 146
Technology
     cultural activists and, 3
     Homer and writing as, *ix*

of Scheherezade II, 74
     writer's choice of, *xi*
That Night in Zyzyzyzyzyyyzzzyyzyzywa, 23–25
THAT WINSOME OTHER ('nym), 19
Thrilling Voice ('nym)
     on role of artistic investigator, 130–131
     on the future, 5
Trial of Tom Robbins
     Another Roadside Attraction dropped
          into water at, 41
     newspaper account, 38–41
     published challenge to Robbins
          before, 36
     saga of, 46–48
Trebay, Guy, 147
Twain, Mark (Samuel Langhorne Clemens), 43

Vernazza, Ani ('nym), 78
Verne, Jules, 102, 103
Vietnam Memorial, 117–118
Vice Editor, The ('nym), 163, 164, 167
Voltaire (François Marie Arouet), 168–169
Vroman, Nicholas, 111

Wolfe, Thomas, 137
Williams, Robin, 153, 154
Winters, Jonathan, 153
Winchell, James, 40, 42, 47
Wittig, Rob, 49, 75
Wohlstetter, Christina, 66
Wohlstetter, Philip, *ix–xi,* 29, 42, 43–44, 75
Wangler, The ('nym), 86
Waste Land, The, 89
Williams, Bill ('nym), 2
Wendy and Tom, 4

Zank, David, 169
Zappa, Frank, 3
Zyzzyzyyzyyzzzyyzyzyzyyzyzyzyyzyzzzwa. *See
     That Night in Zyzzyzyyzyzzzyzyzyywa*

UNIVERSITY PRESS OF NEW ENGLAND
publishes books under its own imprint and is the publisher for Brandeis University Press, Brown
University Press, University of Connecticut, Dartmouth College, Middlebury College Press, University of
New Hampshire, University of Rhode Island, Tufts University, University of Vermont, Wesleyan
University Press, and Salzburg Seminar.

Library of Congress Cataloging-in-Publication Data

Wittig, Rob.
    Invisible rendezvous : connection and collaboration in the new
landscape of electronic writing / Rob Wittig for IN.S.OMNIA.
        p.   cm.
    ISBN 0-8195-5275-5
    1. Computer bulletin boards.   I. IN.S.OMNIA (Computer bulletin
board)   II. Title.
QA76.9.B84W58   1994
818' .5407—dc20

                                                        93-34933